PRINCESS OLGA

PRINCESS OLGA

A WILD AND BAREFOOT ROMANOV

Her Highness
Princess Olga Romanoff

with Coryne Hall

SHEPHEARD-WALWYN (PUBLISHERS) LTD

First published in 2017 by
Shepheard-Walwyn (Publishers) Ltd
107 Parkway House, Sheen Lane,
London SW14 8LS
www.shepheard-walwyn.co.uk

British Library Cataloguing in Publication Data
A catalogue record of this book
is available from the British Library

ISBN: 978 0 85683 517 9

Typeset by Alacrity, Chesterfield, Sandford, Somerset
Printed and bound in the United Kingdom
by Short Run Press, Exeter

*This book is for Nick, Fran and particularly for
my little Poggy who is a brilliant support and help to me.
They all make me laugh and tease me mercilessly!*

ACKNOWLEDGEMENTS

I would like to thank the following for their contributions to the book: Charlotte Ellis, my agent, without whose vision and encouragement this book wouldn't have been written; Coryne Hall for her expert guidance and her extensive knowledge of Romanov history, which has been immensely helpful in providing an accurate historical setting and weaving these into my childhood memories; Preben Ulstrup, who came over from Denmark and helped identify the personages in the photographs and assisted with the captions; and Anthony Werner, my publisher.

CONTENTS

Cast of Main Characters   viii
List of Illustrations   x

 1   The Romanov Legacy   1
 2   My Mother's Family   17
 3   Nursery Days   31
 4   Wild in Kent   47
 5   Out into Society   66
 6   Highland Fling   80
 7   Provender   92
 8   My Children   103
 9   Provender Deteriorates   116
10   Restoration   123
11   Lost Heritage   135
12   Reflections   154

CAST OF MAIN CHARACTERS

My Father's Family, the Romanovs

My great-grandparents:
Tsar Alexander III of Russia
Empress Marie Feodorovna, born Princess Dagmar of Denmark

My grandparents:
Grand Duchess Xenia Alexandrovna (Amama)
Grand Duke Alexander Michaelovich ('Sandro') (Apapa)

My parents:
Prince Andrew Alexandrovich Romanoff
Nadine McDougall

My father's first wife:
Elisabeta Ruffo di Sant' Antimo ('Elsa') (died 1940)

My half siblings:
Princess Xenia ('Mysh') (1919-2000)
Prince Michael (1920-2008)
Prince Andrew (born 1923)

My father's uncles and aunt:
Tsar Nicholas II
Grand Duke Michael Alexandrovich
Grand Duchess Olga Alexandrovna

My father's cousins, children of Nicholas II:
Grand Duchess Olga Nicolaievna
Grand Duchess Tatiana Nicolaievna

Grand Duchess Maria Nicolaievna
Grand Duchess Anastasia Nicolaievna
Tsarevich Alexei Nicolaievich

My father's sister and brothers:
　　Princess Irina ('Aunt Titti'), wife of Prince Felix Yusupov
　　Prince Feodor
　　Prince Nikita
　　Prince Dmitri
　　Prince Rostislav
　　Prince Vassili

My children:
　　Nicholas (Nick)
　　Francis (Fran)
　　Alexandra ('Alex' or 'Poggy')
　　Thomas (Tom, died as a baby)

MY MOTHER'S FAMILY, THE BORGSTRÖMS & THE MCDOUGALLS

My great-grandparents:
　　Emil Borgström
　　Constance Paterson ('Lally')

My grandparents:
　　Sylvia Borgström (divorced)
　　Herbert McDougall

　　Herbert McDougall then married Cicely

My mother and her sisters:
　　Nadine McDougall, wife of Prince Andrew Romanoff
　　Pamela McDougall, wife of George, 4th Earl Sondes
　　Flora McDougall, wife of Jack Kackley (divorced)

LIST OF ILLUSTRATIONS

All illustrations from Princess Olga's collection except 25 and 41

Telegram from the Dowager Empress to Kyrill, 1924   148
Telegram from the Dowager Empress to Grand Duke Nicholas, 1924   148
Letter from the Dowager Empress to Kyrill, 1924   150
First page of Kyrill's letter in reply, 11 October 1924   151

Between pages 68 and 69

1   Princess Olga on the lap of Grand Duchess Xenia
2   Grand Duchess Xenia holding her eldest son, Prince Andrew
3   Grand Duchess Xenia with her son Prince Andrew
4   Grand Duchess Xenia with Princess Irina and Prince Andrew
5   Grand Duke Alexander Michaelovich and Grand Duchess Xenia Alexandrovna with Princess Irina and Prince Andrew
6   Prince Andrew Alexandrovich with some of his siblings and children of neighbouring aristocrats
7   Prince Andrew Alexandrovich in his naval cadet uniform, driving an 'automobile'
8   Prince Rostislav Alexandrovich with his tutor in Grand Duke Alexander's palace
9   Grand Duke Alexander
10   Prince Nikita, Princess Irina, Prince Andrew, Prince Dmitri, Grand Duchess Xenia Alexandrovna, Prince Vassili, Prince Feodor, Prince Rostislav and Grand Duke Alexander Michaelovich
11   The courtyard at Ai-Todor with the 'Old House' and the 'New House'
12   Grand Duke Alexander Michaelovich's Crimean estate, Ai-Todor
13   The children of Grand Duchess Xenia and Grand Duke Alexander
14   Grand Duchess Xenia with her husband, siblings and nieces at Ai-Todor
15   Prince Andrew in his military uniform

16 The Dowager Empress Maria Feodorovna and one of her grandsons

17 The Dowager Empress Maria Feodorovna with her daughter Grand Duchess Xenia and her grandson Prince Nikita

18 Princes Andrew and Feodor at Livadia

19 *HMS Marlborough*, sent by King George V to evacuate the Dowager Empress and her relatives from the Crimea

20 Grand Duchess Xenia Alexandrovna on board *HMS Marlborough* with her granddaughter Princess Irina

21 The Dowager Empress Maria Feodorovna on board *HMS Marlborough* at Yalta

22 Grand Duchess Xenia with her children in exile

23 Grand Duchess Xenia at 'Wilderness House', Hampton Court

24 Prince Felix Felixovich Yusupov and Princess Irina Alexandrovna in exile in France

25 Grand Duke Kyrill Vladimirovich who proclaimed himself 'Emperor'. (Private collection)

26 Prince and Princess Andrew with their daughter, Princess Olga

27 Sister Helen Rowe holding two-month-old Princess Olga

28 Princess Olga aged six or seven months

29 Princess Olga in the pram made by the Queen's coachbuilder

30 Mother Martha with Princess Olga and Prince Andrew

31 Grand Duchess Xenia, Prince Alexander and Princess Margarita von Baden, holding Princess Olga

32 Princess Olga aged 7

33 Princess Olga's 'darling Nanny Ray'

34 Princess Andrew on Chasseur

35 Princess Olga on the donkey Neddy

36 Princess Olga on Tina, the pony on which she learnt to ride

37 Princess Olga and Thomas Mathew after their wedding

38 Princess Andrew with her mother Sylvia McDougall and Grand Duchess Xenia at Craigowan

39 Princess Olga's daughter Alexandra holding her brother Tom, who is holding Oscar

40 Princess Olga's sons Nick and Fran in ATC uniform

41 Princess Olga with Nick, Fran and Alexandra at Banchory. (Courtesy of Aberdeen Press and Journal)

1

THE ROMANOV LEGACY

THERE COULDN'T BE a greater contrast between my upbringing in the wilds of the Kent countryside and my father's childhood in Imperial Russia.

My father, Prince Andrew Romanoff, was the eldest nephew of the murdered Tsar Nicholas II. On my birth certificate his occupation is stated as 'Prince of Russia'. My mother, Nadine McDougall, was my father's second wife, and a member of the wealthy McDougalls flour family.

My childhood was a cross between *The Darling Buds of May* and *Downton Abbey*. I suppose it was an idyllic childhood really.

I was born on 8 April 1950 and grew up at Provender, a historic house parts of which date back to the thirteenth century, near Faversham in Kent. Mother's family, the Borgströms and the McDougalls, had lived there for over a hundred years. I inherited the house when my mother, Nadine, died in 2000.

My earliest memory is of sitting on the rug in what was then the beautiful garden at Provender, then leaning over and picking a daisy. My father was on the grass nearby. After I looked at the flower my parents were encouraging me to crawl over to him. I must have been about six months old.

The paddock in front of the house now was then divided into three paddocks and they were all beautifully maintained. We had geese, donkeys and various other animals in them during my childhood, so I grew up with animals. In fact, I usually got on better with the animals than with the humans!

My father's life in Russia was of course totally different. He was born and brought up in a palace. Before he made his home in England he had already survived the threat of a Bolshevik firing squad. He and his family were lucky that they all managed to get out of Russia alive.

My paternal grandfather was Grand Duke Alexander Michaelovich, known as 'Sandro'. He married Grand Duchess Xenia Alexandrovna, the daughter of Alexander III and his Danish-born wife Dagmar, who became Empress Maria Feodorovna. Alexander and Dagmar had six children: Nicholas II, Alexander who died as a baby, George who died of TB in 1899, my grandmother Xenia, Michael and Olga. Sandro was the grandson of Nicholas I and Xenia was his *great*-granddaughter, so they were first cousins once removed. Sandro, after escaping from the Crimea and settling in France, wrote two very successful books about his life in Russia, *Once a Grand Duke,* and *Always a Grand Duke.*

Xenia and Sandro were married in 1894. Her aunt the Princess of Wales – later Queen Alexandra of Great Britain – came to St Petersburg for the wedding and Queen Victoria sent a present. Every guest received a souvenir – a little purse with the couple's monogram on it, closed by a drawstring and filled with French almonds. Later that year Xenia's father Tsar Alexander III died and her brother Nicholas became the Tsar. Little did 'Nicky' know then the terrible fate that awaited him and his family.

My grandmother had seven children before she was thirty. My grandfather attended all the births, which was very unusual in those days. He was an incredible man, so forward thinking. Apparently, after the revolution even the Soviets had a good opinion of him. He had founded the Russian Air Force, he was Admiral of the Fleet, Minister of Merchant Marine and he even had a club in Paris for the aviators. You name it, Sandro did it.

Their first child was Irina, my Aunt Titti, who was a great beauty and who at the age of eighteen married Prince Felix Yusupov – later to become one of Rasputin's murderers. Xenia had babies every eighteen to twenty months. All the others were boys – my father Andrew, then Feodor, Nikita, Dmitri, Rostislav and Vassili. Childbirth wasn't a problem to her; she just shelled them like peas.

The birth of all these healthy sons upset Empress Alexandra because between 1895 and 1901 she produced only girls who couldn't inherit the throne. When finally a son, Alexei, was born in 1904, he was discovered to be suffering from haemophilia, a disease that prevents the blood from clotting. It could be fatal at any time and the illness was kept a strict secret.

My father was born in the Winter Palace in 1897. He was the only one of Xenia and Sandro's children to have a 21-gun salute to mark his birth. It was unusual – a gun salute was an honour reserved exclusively for the son and heir of the Tsar – but it was done to please Xenia's mother the Dowager Empress. She wanted her eldest grandson to be treated like a Grand Duke.

The birth was late and Nicholas teased Xenia, telling her that only *lady elephants* are pregnant for 22 months! Father was born on January 25th – *our* January 25th – it's something different in the old Julian calendar, in part of the private apartments of the palace because Xenia was caught short. The room had an octagonal ceiling and it used to be Nicholas II's music room. It's sometimes open to the public now when special art exhibitions are housed there.

The windows in the room had two layers of glass, like an early form of double glazing. So my grandfather Sandro wrote the date and time of the birth and the name of the child on the inside of the inner window.

Xenia had seven children between the age of twenty and thirty, which is pretty good. Then after the birth of their last child Sandro started playing around a bit and Xenia took a lover, so they agreed to have a kind of open marriage. Some aristocrats did that once they'd had their children. In fact before the revolution Sandro and Xenia both had long running affairs with a married couple. They used to drive around the south of France in an open car, Sandro and his mistress in the front and her husband and Xenia in the back.

Now the fact that Xenia had a lover was no problem at all. The problem was that the man had been in jail for fraud. He was dodgy. These days nobody would give a monkeys; people go in and out of prison all the time. But it was different in those days. To have a jailbird for a lover wasn't done!

My father and his brothers wore dresses until they were about three years old. In photographs it's very difficult to tell them apart. Again, that's what aristocratic families did – boys and girls were dressed the same.

After their first cosseted years when they were looked after by an English nanny in the nursery, the boys were put into a sailor suit and the regime became a little harsher. Finally, they went through a little more hardship until in the end they were sleeping in a cold dormitory. So they went from one extreme to the other so that they would be tough enough to join their regiment, or the navy. That was how it was done. And Father didn't go to school either; he was educated in the palace by tutors.

He and his cousins were similar ages, so they all played together. A lot has been written about Olga, Tatiana, Maria, Anastasia and Alexei because they were murdered and have since become martyrs. But Pa said they were perfectly normal average kids who just happened to have a Tsar for a father.

They had races with my father and his brothers in the vast corridors of the Winter Palace, and they had bicycle and pony races, roller-skated, climbed trees and played games just like any other cousins. I bet the girls would have practised kissing with their male cousins, because that's what young people did in those days. They were happy, normal children except they were watched and guarded of course – just as Prince George and Princess Charlotte are guarded by royal protection officers now – but in Russia it was the Cossacks who were responsible for the Imperial protection. One of their many problems was that they had a frail mother who used her illness as a power over her children. They were perfectly normal behind their mother's back but the Tsarina became withdrawn from society and frequently used her illness to stop her children doing things that they wanted to do.

Many, many years later I was brought up in a similar way by my mother, who in private always used to make the excuse that her heart was bad. Then she would take to her bed. In this way she'd be completely controlling, but she was a wonderful woman who my friends adored. They would always want to come and talk to 'Auntie Nadine', but she could be very difficult.

So the Tsarina was definitely a control freak. She also controlled Nicholas. For some reason the Romanov men mainly married women with very strong characters who liked to be in control – and the men liked to be dominated. God knows why! It's just one of those things. Nicholas was a darling man whom Pa adored. As he was the eldest nephew, the Tsar used to take him on manoeuvres and Pa would carry the ensign of the regiment.

When the First World War broke out my father was in the Chevalier Guards. Now it was traditional for the Romanov boys, when they reached a certain age, to be sent to a courtesan, not a common whore, to learn how to make love. Making love was a talent, an *art*. It was like painting or music, it wasn't something to be botched. So when the time came they were sent off to the local courtesan – but Father refused to go because he was in love with Elsa, who was to become his first wife, and he was the *faithful* kind of man.

Pa met Elsa when he was about eighteen, or maybe even younger. Her father was Italian, from the Sasso-Ruffo family; her mother was Russian, from the Meshchersky family. Elsa was ten years older than my father. The problem was that she was married to my father's commanding officer and she already had two children by him. But it was all before the days of mobiles, so they would meet when Pa went off on manoeuvres. Pa had been having an affair with her for some time but it was all hushed up. By then he was a lieutenant in the Chevalier Guards but he didn't get his white mess dress because they felt something was afoot. Six months later the revolution broke out.

At the end of 1916, a few months before the revolution, Aunt Titti's husband Felix Yusupov was involved in the murder of Grigori Rasputin. This so-called 'mad Monk' from Siberia had become close to the Tsar and Tsarina as he was the only one who could help Alexei's haemophilia, but a lot of people disliked him and distrusted his influence.

Father liked Rasputin enormously. He said Rasputin wasn't a monk. He didn't bath, he liked to drink, he liked women, he had long hair – but I knew lots of people like that in the sixties. Pa always said Rasputin was a good man and that one day the truth would all come out. He *did* have the power of laying on of hands, which now they call hot hands. His father was also a sort of mystic, a horse whisperer in fact. When a horse was injured, he could lay his hands on the animal and it would recover. That's how the Tsar and Tsarina heard about Rasputin.

Felix, who was bisexual, and his lover Grand Duke Dmitri thought that *they* had murdered Rasputin. Felix invited Rasputin to his private apartment in the basement of the Yusupov Palace with the promise of young girls joining the party – his fondness for female company was well known. They charged the doctor with putting poison in the cakes and wine but Rasputin ate the cakes and drank the wine without anything happening. So, when he got up and started to walk around, Felix shot him, but he still wasn't dead. Then he tried to get out of the palace and was shot again.

I suppose Felix and Dmitri thought he was badly injured and decided to finish him off by drowning him in the River Neva. Having thrown him into the river, they thought they'd done their bit and succeeded in killing him.

But now that the archives are open, it appears that the doctor refused to put the poison in the cakes, which is why they couldn't understand how Rasputin was still walking around the apartment after he'd eaten them. There is also evidence to suggest it was Oswald Rayner from MI6 who shot him and that he was dead by the time he was thrown into the river. Rayner was an old friend of Felix from their time at Oxford University. The British had been tailing Rasputin for a long time because he was allegedly brokering a peace deal between the Germans and the Tsar which would have adversely affected the British.

Felix, however, always maintained *he* had killed Rasputin. He even wrote a book about it. Father was livid and never forgave him for his part in the murder. Incidentally, the room is still furnished as an apartment, with a rather goulish waxwork display of Felix and Rasputin!

A few days before his death, Rasputin was said to have left a letter addressed to the Tsar. He wrote: "if it was your relations who wrought my death then not one of your family, that is to say, none of your children or relations, will remain alive for more than two years. They will be killed by the Russian people…"

Although it's now come out that this story was concocted by Rasputin's secretary, the ominous prediction tragically *did* come true.

In February 1917 the revolution broke out. It started with riots over bread shortages in the capital but soon thousands of workers were marching through the streets holding red banners, chanting, "Down with the government," "Down with the war." Nicholas had gone back to army headquarters, hundreds of miles away. The chief Ministers were mainly the appointees of the Empress (who had been guided by Rasputin) and this was unpopular with the people. The Tsar was urged to return and appoint a Ministry acceptable to the Duma (the Russian parliament) but he didn't realise how serious the situation was and he ignored the pleas for concessions.

When the troops fraternised with the mob, the situation spiralled out of control and, by the time Nicholas decided to return, it was too late. The Imperial Government had collapsed and the railway line to the capital was blocked by revolutionaries. When Nicholas couldn't get back to the capital his train doubled back to Pskov.

Meanwhile Grand Duke Kyrill, who was the tsar's first cousin, had pledged allegiance to the Duma. Father said the Grand Duke had actually marched to the Duma at the head of his regiment of naval guards with a red band on his uniform! Then he returned to his palace and hoisted a red flag on the roof. Pa said Kyrill 'turned turtle' and went from being a White to a Red. He was the first Romanov to break his oath of allegiance to the Tsar. And this was the Tsar's cousin!

Then Nicholas at last agreed to appoint an acceptable ministry but the newly-formed Provisional Government had already decided that he *must* abdicate in favour of Alexei. So on 2 March 1917 Nicholas signed the abdication document in his railway carriage.

It was originally intended that his brother Michael would be regent until 12-year-old Alexei came of age, but Nicholas realised that meant he and Alexandra would be separated from their son. He didn't want that, so he changed his mind and abdicated in favour of Michael.

The next day Michael was told by the Provisional Government that anti-monarchist feeling was high. They couldn't guarantee his safety, so he refused the throne, saying that he would not accept it until asked to by an *elected* Assembly. That was the end of the Romanov dynasty, and Nicholas was brought back to the Alexander Palace at Tsarskoe Selo under arrest.

The British King, George V, was a first cousin of Nicholas II and also, of course, of his sister my grandmother Xenia. They had all been very close ever since they were children, but when the Tsar abdicated

fused to give him asylum. My father always said it was
...inister, Lloyd George, who wouldn't let them come to
...he blamed him. It turns out that this probably was right
...that King George *did* want them to come.

Recently I made a complete idiot of myself crying on national television during a documentary about the Royal House of Windsor. About
four days later a man telephoned me and said, "I was so touched by you
crying on television and I don't want you to feel that George V didn't
try to get your grandmother out of Russia, because he did." This was
just after the revolution, when Xenia was stranded in Petrograd because
all her cars had been requisitioned by the Provisional Government.

And he added: "The reason I know this to be true is because my
grandfather was the officer who was sent from England to rescue your
grandmother from her freezing palace by sledge, along with some of
her children, and to put her on a train to take her to the Crimea, so
that the family were together to be rescued."

The man's grandfather who went out to Russia was a young officer
in the Highland Light Infantry. He could think on his feet without too
much of a problem and he managed to get to Xenia and escort her
down to the Crimea by train. She left the capital towards the end of
March 1917.

He was unable to help poor Tsar Nicholas because he was under
arrest at the Alexander Palace with his family but, thanks to King
George, Xenia was able to join other members of her own family in the
Crimea, which at that time was relatively safe.

It was a secret mission, so even the officer's wife didn't know about
it, but when the officer eventually came back to Britain and told his
wife whom he'd been to rescue, she was not pleased. Xenia was known
to be so beautiful that men fell flat at her feet.

When he came back to London, Lloyd George apparently was livid.
It seems that he didn't really believe in royalty or imperialism and he
definitely didn't want the Romanovs to come to Britain. Later, however,
as the officer's uniform included the wearing of a kilt, King George
presented him with a dirk – a ceremonial dagger – in recognition of
his service.

According to this man's grandfather, there was also a suspicion at
the time that M15 had been penetrated by a mole sympathetic to the

Bolshevik cause. Anything written had to be in code to preserve total secrecy.

In the Royal Archives there is indeed a letter from George V to Lloyd George that says the Romanovs must not be allowed to come to England. It was shown in the television programme. The man on the telephone explained that King George was persuaded to write that letter to Lloyd George rescinding permission because of the threat posed by the mole. It put King George and his family in a very difficult position.

All this happened at the time the King was trying to make the royal family 'user-friendly' to the British people by replacing the Royal Family's German name of Saxe-Coburg-Gotha with the more English-sounding 'House of Windsor'. There was a lot of anti-German feeling in Britain at the time, with shop windows being broken and dachshunds stoned in the streets, and the problem was that, although Nicholas's wife Alexandra was Queen Victoria's granddaughter, she *was* German and the British didn't want *her* to come to this country. That's what I was always told, anyway. Also, the British didn't want an influx of the Romanovs because they were a *huge* family.

With no rescue in sight, the Tsar and his family were sent to Tobolsk in Siberia in the summer of 1917. Of course everyone hoped they would escape. So when later that year a telegram from Edinburgh was delivered to the Tsarina's sister Victoria, Marchioness of Milford Haven, saying "Tatiana has arrived!" it caused great excitement. The family initially took it to mean that the Tsar's daughter had escaped from captivity, but in fact the telegram was from Victoria's son George and his wife, announcing the birth of their daughter.

Lenin's seizure of power in October 1917 was the death-knell for the Romanovs. The Tsar and his family were murdered by the Bolsheviks the following year. I don't know any more about what happened in July 1918 than is generally known. My father was none the wiser either. No one knows exactly what happened, apart from the people who carried out the murders.

At the time when the Tsar and his family were killed, my father, my grandmother and my *great*-grandmother Dagmar were all in Yalta, hundreds of miles away from Ekaterinburg, which is in the foothills of the Urals as you're going to Siberia. It took a few weeks for the news that they had been murdered to filter through to them. What *actually* happened I don't think anyone will really know, but we *do* know that they were murdered. My great-grandmother would never admit that this atrocity had happened. She would never ever talk about it, and if ever it was mentioned she said that the Russians would never murder her son, the Tsar. Many other Grand Dukes were also murdered, but their fate is not talked about so much and modern Russians didn't hear anything about it until quite recently. My father's uncle Michael, the Tsar's brother, was shot in Perm in 1918. Then, on my grandfather's side, my father's uncle Grand Duke Sergei Michaelovich was murdered at around the same time at Alapayevsk, also in the Urals. He was thrown down a mineshaft with other members of his family. My father lost two more uncles, shot by a firing squad in early 1919.

Meanwhile, my father's family and some of their cousins were under house arrest in the Crimea for eight months. For part of the time they were in my grandfather Sandro's own home, Ai-Todor.

What I didn't realise was that, before they were arrested, Papa used to go up to the capital (which had been renamed Petrograd) incognito from the Crimea to see what was going on in the palaces. He went several times. Prince Felix Yusupov also travelled there to hide jewels and artworks in his own palaces in the hope of getting it all back later. He and Pa didn't travel together though, as Felix was too well-known. Pa could just go under the radar.

While they were under arrest my great-grandmother Dagmar, Empress Maria Feodorovna, kept a diary. It was something she had done for years. Amongst the incidents recorded – she told how suddenly one night sailors poured into her bedroom at Ai-Todor showing no respect. She heard a voice telling her to get out of bed. It was an officer of the new Provisional Government who wanted to search her room to find compromising documents that they were convinced she had hidden there.

Dagmar wrote in detail about the disrespectful attitude of these people, especially one of the women. She called this woman the worst possible things – she even tore away the mattress to search for papers hidden inside. Then the officer looked in the drawers of her writing table. They took documents from her on that occasion and also her old diaries, but not her jewellery box. Sitting in her chair she would hide it under her skirts when the Bolsheviks came. They never found it.

Early in 1918 they were moved to the nearby palace of Djulber under guard, about to be shot by the Bolsheviks at any second. They only escaped the firing squad because that part of the Crimea was overrun by the Germans. Otherwise they would definitely have all perished.

In April 1919 George V sent *HMS Marlborough* to the Crimea to rescue my grandmother Xenia, great grandmother Dagmar, my uncles and Aunt Titti. They managed to get out just before the Bolsheviks retook the area.

There was a man called Zadorojny who was in charge while they were under house arrest. When the Bolsheviks came to shoot the Romanovs he always made up excuses as to why that day wasn't right for the executions and sent them away again. But years later, Papa was made President of the *Chaine des Rotisseurs,* an International Association of Gastronomy, and one of the people there was Jewish. He told Papa that Zadorojny was well-known to them as a hero for saving the lives of that branch of the Imperial family.

My grandfather Sandro, my father and Elsa left Russia on *HMS Forsythe* four months before the rest of the family. At some point Elsa's husband had either died or they had divorced, sources differ on this point, but by November 1918 she was around five months pregnant by Pa. They married in November in the chapel at Ai-Todor, which was all quite romantic, but my great-grandmother refused to go to the wedding. The following month Pa and Elsa sailed to France with Sandro to try and drum up support for the White Russian army, which of course as we all know now failed.

They never realised that was the end. Papa really believed that this was going to be a temporary glitch and they would be back in Russia. As time rolled on, my great-grandmother, grandmother and all the others also realised things were rather dire. My grandmother's sister Grand Duchess Olga Alexandrovna got out of Russia a different way because she had married a commoner just before the revolution.

Her married name was Kulikovsky and the Bolsheviks no longer recognised that she was a Romanov, so she was off the Soviet hit list, unlike the others. The same goes for Aunt Titti, whose married name was Yusupov. But any Grand Duke or Duchess was about to be shot. Olga was an artist. She had two boys with Colonel Kulikovsky and died in Canada in 1960. Their great-grandson and I sometimes see each other in Russia, and Fran, one of my sons, is in touch with him quite a lot.

My grandfather Sandro *never* came to England after the revolution. As I said, the government here wasn't keen on being overrun by Romanov Grand Dukes and by that time my grandparents were amicably separated. Not by law, but they'd had their lovers and just came to an agreement. Sandro was extremely angry at the way the British treated Nicholas and everybody else. He was a very close advisor of the Tsar and wrote him a letter just before the revolution saying, "You're making a terrible mistake..." but Nicholas wouldn't listen.

Sandro, who spoke many languages, was very happy to remain in France, which was perfect. But Xenia did go and see him when he was ill. He died of spinal cancer, but she went to the South of France so that she could be with him during that period. They remained close. He and Xenia are buried in Roquebrune Cemetery, which apparently overlooks a bay in the south of France. I've never been there but it's a special cemetery where many Russians are buried and their graves are together. It's rather a pretty place, because it's got mimosa bushes and plants around the cemetery.

Pa was twenty-one when he arrived in France. Shortly afterwards he became a father when my half-sister Xenia was born in Paris. So Pa had three children before he was twenty-five – Xenia, Michael and Andrew, all very close together in age – and then he had me with his second wife when he was fifty-four.

Quite a lot of the entourage who worked for them had left Russia on the *Marlborough* or the *Forsythe*, so they had the nannies. They looked after the children, so my father and Elsa went out to parties or functions at the embassies. They socialised a lot, so didn't spend much time with the children, as was the custom for upper class families then. He and Elsa were very happy though.

They remained in Paris for a while. But although Pa was a Russian prince he had to earn a living. Luckily he was *very* creative, so they opened a shop designing handbags, scarves and costume jewellery. In fact it was a little more elaborate than ordinary costume jewellery as he would use lapis lazuli and other semi precious stones, but it certainly wasn't Fabergé. I still have the book of his designs.

At first the shop was very successful, they were making quite a lot of money and it was all going swimmingly. Then Papa's silent partner ran away with the takings, so they came to England when their eldest son Michael was born.

I *think* Pa started the business all over again somewhere in London, but I don't think it lasted very long. I believe the same thing happened, and allegedly the partner ran off with the takings. Of course Pa knew nothing about money because he had never had to carry any. In Russia such matters were taken care of by staff.

King George V was *wonderful* to my grandmother Xenia. Queen Mary wasn't keen on George and Xenia being so close. She might have been a little jealous, but the cousins had known each other since nursery days. My grandmother was George's favourite cousin.

I know my father was in awe of Queen Mary. And I think he *liked* her. She did quite a lot of good things during the war, like turning up on bomb sites and visiting factories. George and Mary were brave – they didn't get up and leave Buckingham Palace.

Queen Mary had a rather annoying habit though. She would go to a dinner party and the hosts would seat her on the best Sheraton chair. There were maybe eleven more chairs around the table. During dinner she'd say: "*Oh*, I *do* like this chair." And the hosts felt obliged to give her the whole set of twelve. When she'd come to tea she would say, "Oh, gosh that jug's beautiful! I've got one like that and it would be so nice to have a pair…" and the people would resist. But she'd sit there till seven o'clock, and in the end they had to give it to her to get rid of her.

People got wise to this and when she was visiting they would put their *best* things into the attic and bring out their *second* best. She was well known for it. One day Queen Mary showed Xenia a beautiful Fabergé rose jade box with a diamond and emerald monogram above the Imperial crown, which she had just acquired. "I would be interested to know whose initials those are," she said. Xenia looked at the entwined 'K.A.' and said, "They are mine."

Allegedly there's a room at Buckingham Palace, which isn't on view, which was once Queen Mary's room. It is crammed full of stuff she 'collected' from the houses she stayed in or visited, but nobody knows who it all belongs to because they're all dead now.

During the Second World War Queen Mary went to stay with her niece the Duchess of Beaufort at Badminton with an entourage of *sixty* people. Admittedly the house *was* an estate, so it was self-sufficient and had its own herd of cows and other animals Still, she didn't put her hand in her pocket once.

Once Pa and Elsa came to England, they never left. They lived with my grandmother, because George V had granted Xenia a grace and favour home, Frogmore Cottage, which is actually a rather large house near Windsor Castle.

My youngest half brother Andrew wrote a book called *The Boy Who Would be Tsar*. In it he tells how one Easter an enormous chocolate egg was delivered to Frogmore Cottage from Fortnum's or Harrods. It was an absolutely beautiful Easter Egg and he and his siblings soon devoured it. Shortly afterwards a flunky knocked on the door. "I think an Easter Egg might have been delivered here in error. It should have gone to the castle. It was meant for Princess Elizabeth and Princess Margaret." Whereupon the person who opened the door had to admit, "I'm so sorry, but the children ate it all."

Just before the Second World War my grandmother was granted another grace and favour home, Wilderness House at Hampton Court Palace. Father and Elsa moved in there with her.

On 29 October 1940 the house was bombed during the blitz and the windows were shattered. Elsa, who had been suffering from cancer of the rectum for some time, died that day. She was only fifty-one. The funeral service was held in the chapel at Wilderness House and she was buried in Old Windsor cemetery.

My half-brothers joined the navy in the Second World War and they both saw lots of action. The eldest one Michael was an officer, and was an aeronautical tool engineer on one of the famous aircraft carriers. Andrew joined as a rating and for some reason never became an officer. I don't think he wanted to. I know he went to officer school because I've found his letters, but he quite enjoyed his life as a rating. He spent a very active war up in Scapa Flow in Scotland, amongst other places, and then at some point joined the action.

The two different ships the brothers were on happened to be in Hong Kong at the same time and they met. So one day Michael, the officer, took his brother, whom he hadn't seen for three years or so, to the Officers' club. That caused a *huge* hoo-ha. He was rapped over the knuckles and evicted because he'd brought a mere *rating* – even though it was his brother – into the Officers' club!

When the war ended, Michael was de-mobbed in Australia. He had three wives – two were Australian and one an Australian-Italian – and spent the rest of his life in Australia. Occasionally he travelled abroad. Sadly he died in Sydney in 2008. Andrew emigrated to the States when he was quite young. On the back of his book *The Boy Who Would Be Tsar* is a photograph of a telegram from my parents dated 4 February 1949, wishing him luck. He visited England a few times but never came back permanently. Andrew also married three times and was the only one of my siblings who had children. He married a Russian woman and divorced. Then he married an American woman and was widowed. Then he married for a third time. He is ninety-five now and lives in California.

My half-sister Xenia was known as Mysh, because she looked like a mouse when she was born. *Mysh* is mouse in Russian. People used to mistake her for my father's sister because Papa was only just twenty-two when she was born. She had very dark hair, chain smoked *Gauloise* and *Disque* Bleu and sounded foreign too.

My poor sister used to get tortured by the old *Babushkas*, the servants who came out on the *Marlborough* with them and looked after my grandmother, because they said it was *her* fault that Papa *had* to marry Elsa. I remember Mysh saying they were quite cruel to her, really mean and nasty.

Another person who was sometimes unkind to my sister when they were at the same parties, although she was a lot younger than Mysh, was Princess Margaret.

Mysh trained as a nurse at Great Ormond Street Hospital and to supplement her income she modelled for Elizabeth Arden. In those days Elizabeth Arden made clothes as well as make up and they approached Mysh and asked her to model for them. She was photographed in *Tatler* and other glossy magazines – she was a good model.

Mysh was married by the time I came along. Most of the time she was really nice but she and my mother didn't get on. The first man she married was an American from the US Army – Calhoun Ancrum from South Carolina – and they divorced quite soon afterwards.

Then she married a lovely man called Dr Geoffrey Tooth, who at some point was the head of the mental side of the Ministry of Health under Enoch Powell. He was the same age as my mother. They lived in England until he retired, then they bought a barn in France. While they renovated the place they lived on their boat in a creek in Britain and then they moved permanently to France. They both loved France, and stayed there until they died.

After Wilderness House was bombed in 1940 my father and grand-mother went up to Scotland to get away from the blitz. King George VI lent them Craigowan, a house on the Balmoral estate where Prince Charles and his first wife Diana spent a lot of time. It was while he was living in Scotland that Father met my mother again.

2

MY MOTHER'S FAMILY

MY MOTHER'S FAMILY was of Scottish and Scandinavian descent. Though over a thousand miles separated my parents' birthplaces and their backgrounds were widely different, there had been some strange coincidences in the two families' past, where fate brought them together. But more of that later.

My mother was Nadine McDougall. The head of the Clan McDougall lived at Dunollie Castle near Oban on the west coast of Scotland. It's a ruin now. My branch of the McDougalls came from the Scottish Borders.

The McDougall Mills were founded by my grandfather's grandfather Alexander McDougall. He was responsible for bringing white flour and white bread to Britain. So maybe in taking the goodness out of it to make the flour white, he's guilty of bringing obesity to the nation as well! Curiously, one day a man came to the docks and saw the piles of brown husks that were being taken out of the flour. He recognised their value and offered to buy them. This, of course, is wheat germ from which Bemax is made. The firm is still going.

Alexander's brother was a chemical engineer. Among other things he invented sheep dip and founded a company that became Cooper McDougall.

So the McDougalls made their fortune through flour and chemical inventions. They were landowners and owned a house called St. Rhadagunds in Ventnor on the Isle of Wight where my mother and her sisters would stay with their grandmother every year. The family also had property at Blackheath, in London.

My maternal grandfather Lieutenant Colonel Herbert McDougall was one of twelve children. In those days, if you could afford it, and the McDougalls certainly could, you just bred. Herbert had quite a colourful life. He lied about his age so he could join the army. He fought in the Boer War, then in the First World War and commanded the Natal Mounted Rifles in South Africa during the Second World War. He was also the last member of the family who actually *worked* in the flour mills.

His brother Arthur McDougall owned a hotel called Skindles at Maidenhead, which is no longer there. Sadly he was an alcoholic, but he was a lovely man, and very generous to his nieces. When my mother got married he bought her wedding dress, and did the same for her younger sister. He also gave Mother some beautiful jewels, including the most amazing pink sapphire ring. Sadly, they are long gone ...

My other great-grandmother, on my mother's maternal side, was also born and brought up in Scotland. She was Constance Paterson of Castle Huntly, Dundee. The Patersons had a long history of military service; from father to son they commanded their regiments.

I was told that in 1854 during the Crimean War, my Paterson great-great-grandfather commanded his regiment at Balaclava against the army of my Russian great-great-great-grandfather Tsar Nicholas I. It was also a Paterson who was involved in founding the Bank of England in the 1690s. This was William Paterson, who must have been my great-great-great-great-great-uncle.

Constance Paterson married Emil Borgström, who was a Swedish-Finn. At that time Finland was part of the huge Russian Empire. The Tsar of Russia was also the ruler of Finland. Tsar Alexander I had annexed Finland in 1809 during the wars against Sweden. The border was only twenty-five miles from St Petersburg and the Tsar ruled as Grand Duke of Finland. In 1812 he moved the capital from Åbo to Helsingfors (now Helsinki) on the Gulf of Finland and confirmed that Finland's privileges established under Swedish rule would be maintained.

But relations between Finland and Russia were not always easy, especially after later rulers started on a programme of Russification, insisting that the Russian language be used in all Finnish institutions and that the postal and conscription laws be brought into line with those of Russia.

My paternal great-grandparents, Tsar Alexander III and Tsarina Maria Feodorovna, called Dagmar, liked Finland so much that they had a fishing lodge built at the Langinkoski rapids near Kotka so they could spend a few weeks there every summer. It was all very informal. They chopped their own wood, did their own cooking and the children slept in a dormitory.

In Finland in those days the ruling classes all spoke Swedish, so Scandinavian-born Dagmar was able to go and chat to the local people. Now the Swedish-speaking Finns are in the minority and it's compulsory to learn Finnish at school.

The Borgströms were hugely wealthy and very powerful. Emil's father, my great-great-grandfather Henrik Borgström, was born in a place called Borgå in Finland and next door in the same little town was the house where my great-great-great-uncle Tsar Alexander I of Russia stayed in 1809. I went to Borgå and saw their houses. What a strange coincidence that my two ancestors, on my mother's side and on my father's side, were once neighbours and knew each other over 200 years ago!

Helsinki, as it is now, is due largely to the Borgströms. Henrik founded the first private bank in Finland, the first railway, and created the great parks of the city which he gave to the nation. He was also responsible for importing tobacco to Finland. There are statues of him in Helsinki.

Ironic really that with all these banks in my family I have no wealth to show for it!

There have been other twists of fate between my mother's family and the Romanovs, generations before my parents married. Henrik Borgström's son Emil, who was first Secretary at the Finnish Embassy in St James's in London, and his wife Constance Paterson produced four children, one of whom was my grandmother Sylvia.

Sylvia and her twin sister Léonie were debutantes at the court of St Petersburg where they were presented to my paternal great-grandfather Alexander III at the Winter Palace. Who would have guessed then, that the descendants of these two powerful families, the Romanovs and the Borgströms, would marry one day, and their lives would be intertwined forever?

Sadly, Constance was widowed young, when Emil died very suddenly. She went into deep mourning after his death, and rather like Queen Victoria after the death of Prince Albert, never got out of black. She came back to Britain from Finland because she wanted to be near her sister. The sister was married to an Emeritus Professor of Astronomy at Cambridge University who also happened to be the Vicar at Murston in Kent just up the road from Provender. He knew the house and at his suggestion Constance rented Provender from 1890, until her daughter Sylvia, my grandmother, bought the house in 1912 where I still live today.

My maternal grandparents also had a wild streak. Sylvia Borgström and Herbert McDougall met while hunting with the local hunt, the Tickham. *All* the McDougall girls – and boys – hunted down here in Kent because the Tickham Hunt was so good. My grandpa McDougall was in the musketry school at Hythe, so he knew the area before he eloped with my grandmother.

The story of their elopement is quite romantic. My great-grandmother Constance had a suitable young man lined up for Sylvia, who by that time was quite *old* for a girl to be still unmarried. In those days girls were supposed to be married before they reached their twenties, but of course Sylvia was Finnish so it was slightly different.

Early in 1906 Sylvia and her mother were having tea at one of the big hotels in London, probably Claridges, before continuing their journey to Tilbury. There they were to catch the ship that would take them to Finland so that Great-granny could marry her off to the suitable young man she had lined up. But my grandfather had a bold plan. He sent his best friend, a man called Tudor Barr, to find Sylvia and hand her a note. She read it and said to her mother, "Oh, I'll be back in a minute," and rushed outside where Grandpa was waiting for her with a coach and horses. She got in, and they galloped down to Kent. He'd got a special licence, so they were married straightaway in Lynsted Church, which is five miles from Provender.

In those days the Borgströms were *terrible* snobs. They thought that my grandfather McDougall, a miller – a *miller!* – wasn't a suitable husband for Constance. The Borgströms were much more snobbish then than they are now. Anyway, it all turned out all right, except that eventually my grandparents divorced.

After Herbert and Sylvia were married, they lived in the lovely house he had rented called Loyterton. He learnt to farm, because that's what gentlemen did in those days. Lewis Finn, an old friend of the family and owner of a big estate, taught him all about farming, rather like going to Cirencester Agricultural College. In fact we're still friends with the same family. Nearby there was a big house called Mount Ephraim which had a round drive, so they used to have dog-cart races and bet on who could go around the fastest.

My grandfather became a successful farmer in a small way. He played polo and had his own polo field on the farm. He was very generous and had a wicked sense of humour. There was a story of how, way back when he was still married to Granny, he was at home in his den smoking a cigar, when the maid knocked on the door and said: "Colonel, there is a gentleman to see you at the front door."

Grandpa got up and went to see who the gentleman was. It turned out to be an old tramp. He gave him some money and sent him on his way. When he came back inside, he said to the maid: "Next time the Duke calls tell him I'm out!"

By the time Mother was six years old, Herbert and Sylvia had given up Loyterton farmhouse and moved in with my great-grandmother Constance at Provender. That would be around 1914, so my mother and her sisters lived here when they were little. The children couldn't pronounce 'Granny', so they called her Lally. Eventually Lally came round to the idea that her son-in-law wasn't so bad after all. When she went blind he'd sit and read stories to her.

Lally remained at Provender until she died in 1915. She had a full staff. There were two footmen, a butler, a cook, tweenies, a kitchen maid, a scullery maid, a coachman and lots of gardeners and garden boys. My mother always told me that when Grandpa still lived up the road at Loyterton before the First World War he used to walk about a mile over the fields to Provender with his three daughters – although I think that only my mother was old enough actually to walk over at the time. Granny was away a lot so he used to get the children to Provender somehow to visit their grandmother, his mother-in-law Constance. He always thought it was ridiculous that *one* woman lived in such a large house with all that staff.

When war broke out all the male staff had to go off to fight, unless they were too old or unfit. With no male help, everyone had to muck in. My grandmother had Jersey cows, enough to produce all the cream and milk they needed. Granny converted the brewery to a dairy and she would milk the cows and then make the butter herself. It didn't last for a *very* long time, but she was quite able to do it. Of course, with the war on, all the comfort and luxury they were used to had gone, as it had for most houses in Britain.

Herbert's mother, my McDougall great-grandmother Margaret, had a beautiful big house in Blackheath which was called Dunollie, after Dunollie Castle. She was born Margaret McCree. *Her* great-great-grandmother had stitched an embroidery sampler in the 1600s, which is now in the children's room at Provender with the name McCree.

During part of the First World War Margaret McDougall rented a house in Blackheath for her daughter-in-law Sylvia, so that she could come and stay there with her children – my mother and her sisters – while Herbert was away at war. The house was on a corner. I still see it when I drive into London from Kent.

Mother remembered Blackheath being totally wild. Every day the nanny would walk them to the little pond and then they'd sail boats and walk back home. At that time the transport was mainly horse-drawn vehicles because they were saving fuel for the war. She thought it was really lovely. Regrettably it's not like that any more and I don't even know if Dunollie is still standing. There are great big housing estates all over that area now.

My mother had two sisters. My youngest aunt, Flora, liked to travel, so from the age of fifteen she travelled a lot with either my grandfather or my grandmother. She *loved* Finland. My grandmother's twin sister Léonie was a writer and she had bought the property of Hammarborg on an island in the Finnish archipelago of Barösund. When she died she left it to my grandmother, Sylvia, who then gave it to Flora in 1955. To get to their Finnish Island, Flora and her daughter Diana had to take a train through Soviet territory or drive for six hours around the Russian part. Barösund wasn't under Russian control, but the Soviets still had a huge chunk of the land around it.

Flora married an American called John Kackley who had an important position in the American Navy and served at the American Embassy in London during the Second World War. Flora and Jack had one child. She divorced him later, because there were various flaws in the marriage, and changed her name to Kaley. She came back to England for a while and then moved to Italy. My cousin Diana was brought up and went to school there and took her M.A. in Rome. She's a little older than me and speaks five languages.

The middle sister, Pamela, became Countess Sondes and died of ovarian cancer in 1967 when she was in her early fifties. Those were the days of the Maharishi Mahesh Yogi, the Guru at whose feet the Beatles used to sit. He brainwashed Pamela into believing that you could heal things by thought alone, so she totally ignored her cancer symptoms. By the time they opened her up it had spread everywhere. Her son Henry also died of cancer in his early fifties; he was ten years older than me. Henry had enormous charm and women fell flat at his feet.

When Mother was about twenty her parents divorced. My grandmother says in her autobiography that her husband liked 'to chase petticoats'. This was her *kind* way of saying he got his leg over every other female. So they divorced because Granny preferred writing books and travelling, and Grandpa liked the women. I think it was all fairly amicable. He was generous to his children and his ex-wife. He always looked after them well – until he had a new family to support.

Apparently at one time, between his first and second marriages, he had *six* 'Mrs McDougalls' in London. That's some going!

Three years after the divorce, he married his second wife, Cicely, who was more than thirty years younger than him. She was South African, so they moved to Natal. Grandpa was too old by then to fight in the Second World War, but he commanded the Natal Mounted Rifles. They came back to England after the war and bought a big house called Cawston Manor, at Cawston in Norfolk. The estate had a big lake and he used to organise shoots on the estate. I remember going there a couple of times as a very small child.

When Grandpa married this much younger woman he produced two sons. In those days inheritance was done by primogeniture, which meant that the eldest son inherited, so the girls didn't get the money they thought they might get from Grandpa.

After her divorce, Granny McDougall renounced her Lutheran faith and converted to Catholicism. The local Catholic priest was Father Lynch, who came from a famous Irish priestly family. He always said that if he'd got to Granny *before* the divorce there would never have been a divorce. She certainly became a *devout* convert to Catholicism.

Granny travelled a lot while she was researching and writing her books. She wrote ten or more, and some of them were bestsellers. The last one was her autobiography *Let's Light the Candles*, which was highly acclaimed and won awards. It was published in 1944, before I was born, hence the dedication "To my two grandchildren – Henry and Diana." She wrote under a man's name, Paul Waineman, because she believed a book by a woman wouldn't sell unless it was by Jane Austen.

She also wrote travel novels and Barbara Cartland type books, the sort of frothy romance where the boys *never* got their leg over the girls because they were all virgins. It paid well, and as she was hard up, she needed to work. Writing books was her occupation and she was good at it.

I haven't read *Let's Light the Candles* for a long while, partly because she was the most *dreadful* snob and would say things in a way that makes me want to scream. She refers to her daughters as Princess Andrew and Countess Sondes, but can't quite get her tongue round the fact that her youngest child married a chap from the navy.

Mother travelled quite a lot herself. She bred red setters and used to do field-trial championships up in the north of Scotland. She didn't get married until she was thirty-four.

She first met my father at the Finnish Embassy in London before the war. She wasn't a debutante but Granny sent her to smart parties, including the embassy, because she thought it was a way for her to learn correct behaviour in a social setting. Mother became an *expert* on etiquette. She would stand in a line-up and kiss Pa's hand and then that of his wife Elsa – everyone bowed and curtseyed. Eventually, after doing this many times over several months, she was told by Elsa not to bother with the protocol any more.

At the end of 1940 Elsa died of cancer and my father joined his mother, Grand Duchess Xenia, at Craigowan on the Balmoral Estate. There's a hotel north of Banchory, the Raemoir House Hotel, which has my grandmother Xenia's signature in its old visitors' book. When they were on their way to Balmoral it was one of the many places they would stay.

At that time my McDougall grandmother and my mother were staying in Aboyne while Granny was writing another book. So my parents met again at parties on Deeside.

Mother was doing her bit for the war by driving trucks for the Canadians, and they would tease her, saying, "Oh gee, you know that the prince is in love with you!"

"Oh don't be ridiculous," Mother would reply. But he was and he proposed in the woods at Balmoral.

There was a gypsy's prediction, made after they met again, but a good time before my father asked her to marry him. Mother had gone off to see a gypsy fortune-teller above the fish market in Aberdeen. I only know what my mother told me but obviously the fortune-teller must have told her a lot more.

The gypsy said, "Oh, you're going to meet a tall, dark, handsome man."

Mother thought, "Yeah, that's what they always say."

"And when he proposes, he's going to give you an enclosed crown with a red ruby in it. This man is related to all the royal houses of Europe," the gypsy went on, and Mother thought, "Rubbish! Typical gypsy talk."

When she went back to her mother in Aboyne, which is only about thirty-five minutes from Aberdeen, she asked her. "Which ruling house has an enclosed crown with a red ruby?"

As mentioned earlier, Finland was once ruled by Russia, so the Tsar was my maternal grandmother's sovereign as well. So my grandmother said to my mother: "Oh, you silly girl! That's the Imperial house of the Romanovs of course."

A year or so later my father took my mother on a picnic in the woods at Balmoral and asked her to marry him. He put his hand in his inner pocket – and she told him exactly what he was going to pull out!

Although Pa spoke five languages, his English accent was very poor at times. "*Funtastik!*" he said, as he pulled out the enclosed crown with the red ruby in it. Later the gypsy contacted Mother again and asked her to come back, because she could tell her more about her future and her offspring. But my grandmother Xenia persuaded her not to go.

Xenia had a terrible time all her life with her husband Sandro because he had second sight. Not that he dabbled in anything sinister or the occult, but she found it very difficult to deal with his mysticism. That's why she pleaded with my mother: "Please don't go and see the gypsy again, I've had so much trouble in my life with Sandro." So Mother never went back.

Sandro was indeed a clairvoyant. Once he was on manoeuvres on the other side of Russia. There were no mobiles then, no proper telephones, the distance was huge and getting hither and thither was a real task. While there he was invited into the house of a merchant who had the most amazing collection of coins. Sandro also collected coins. "Gosh," he said, "I really would like to buy those, they look fantastic, but I don't have money on me. They would look good in my collection though."

And the man said, "Please, have them. I'll give them to you."

"Absolutely no way, I'm not taking them," replied Sandro.

When Sandro went back to St Petersburg and as he was sitting at his desk thinking about the coins – they suddenly appeared on his desk! I think that's called teleportation. So he had to send them back again.

Later when he was in France, after his memoirs were published, he wrote books on mysticism and also went on lecture tours in America. I'd like to have met Sandro. He died in 1933 before I was even thought of.

My parents married in Kent on 21 September 1942, but because of the war it was a small wedding and Xenia was unable to come since travelling down from Scotland was too difficult.

They had two services, one Anglican and the other Russian Orthodox. My grandfather Herbert McDougall was in South Africa by then, so my great-uncle Arthur McDougall gave Mother away at the first ceremony in St Mary's, Norton. The Archbishop of Canterbury officiated and Pa's brother Dmitri was best man. Mother had a traditional wedding dress of white satin with a train, and a Russian style *kokoshnik* head-dress of pearls holding her veil. According to *The Times* she had three pages, Jeremy Lee Pemberton (Lord Kingsdown's brother who is still alive), Robert Mercer, and her two-year-old nephew Henry, Viscount Throwley. Going up the aisle the little boy was supposed to be carrying the train, but he just stood still, and said, "I'm not going." His nanny had to prod the little dear.

About half an hour later there was a second ceremony at Sheldwich Church according to the Orthodox rites, by special permission of the Archbishop of Canterbury. According to my grandmother's autobiography, "it was the first time that an Orthodox rite had been held in an English parish church". For this ceremony Mother was given away by Sir Robert Hodgson, Dmitri acted as one of the crown bearers and the Archimandrite Nicholas officiated. Before converting to Orthodoxy, the Archimandrite had been Charles Sydney Gibbes, tutor to Pa's cousins, the Tsar's children.

After a reception at Lees Court they spent the first night of their honeymoon at Skindles in Maidenhead, then went up to Craigowan. When my parents were walking around the Balmoral estate they had to find out whether they were going to bump into any members of the Royal family. They couldn't just wander in the woods; they had to get permission at certain times. If they did happen to bump into anyone they'd have to get off the track and Pa would bow and my mother would curtsey. It was etiquette. The present Queen would be there sometimes. She was a teenager then, but occasionally they would run into her and Mother would curtsey.

Queen Elizabeth (later the Queen Mother) had been very fond of Elsa and used to visit her. But Pa didn't ask her permission for his second marriage, which he should have done out of courtesy according to etiquette. Allegedly, this offended Queen Elizabeth and the doors closed. That's what Papa told me.

My parents came back to Kent but they couldn't live at Provender, because during the war it was requisitioned by the army. The officers lived in the house and the men lived in the Nissan huts they built in the back field. So Ma and Pa rented part of a house in Lynsted that looked just like Provender. It was very haunted – so I was told by my parents and particularly by the maid who worked there.

Father joined the Home Guard, like Captain Mainwaring's lot in *Dad's Army*. Pa was very deaf but he was also very brave. So when everybody else was ducking for cover, Pa could be seen in the village walking along the pavement with the shrapnel zooming around his head. He enjoyed that. I'm sure if he'd been younger he would have happily joined the army.

Mother's beautiful sister Pamela and her husband George lived six miles away at Lees Court, a huge, grand old house with over thirty bedrooms. The military had also requisitioned it but the family were allowed to keep a wing. My half-brothers used to come to stay with Pa when they were on leave and Pamela had an affair with one of them while George was away doing his bit for his country. He just put a ladder up against the window and climbed in. When Mother found out that her step-son had been having a fling with her sister she was absolutely livid.

Towards the end of the war the military left and the family moved back to Provender. Granny moved back first with Aunt Flora to do the cleaning-up and see the damage, which was great both in the house and in the completely-wrecked garden. The officers were apparently totally ignorant. Mother turned up one day to find them sluicing down the gallery with buckets and a broom, like you'd do on the deck of a ship. And then they were getting into her cupboards, even though they were secured with Bramah locks, and doing charades in her clothes. She wasn't happy.

I still have all the letters and receipts from the War Office. They had to pay a *lot* of money to repair it all.

Pa was brought to Provender because as an impoverished prince who'd lost everything, he had no money and nowhere to live. But he loved this place. He absolutely adored it. And he felt safe here.

There was talk that the Soviets were still after the Russian aristocracy, even after all this time. Mother was nervous. Throughout her married life she was always being invited to visit her family in Finland but she wouldn't go back, because it used to be ruled by Russia and Russia was so *close* to Finland. She was too scared of Papa being captured, or herself being captured, even though the family had changed the spelling of their name in exile from Romanov to Romanoff. Pa said it was a much more common name in Russia, like Smith is in Britain, but Mother was still scared that they might be on Stalin's hit list.

In fact it turns out that she had good reason to be worried, because in the 1930s the Soviets were kidnapping former White Russian generals off the streets in Paris. The fact that the Soviets were active in Paris had sent the Russian community there into a panic and many of Pa's relatives hired their own private security. Amama – my grandmother Xenia – was on Stalin's hit list for a long time, but she was protected by the British at her Grace-and-Favour houses – first at Frogmore, then at Wilderness House.

My father would love to have gone on a plane and flown somewhere, but my mother wouldn't get on a plane, she'd never flown. Poor Pa was *desperate* to fly. But apart from going to France for the funeral of his mother and various other family members, he never left England.

About two years after her marriage, around 1944, Mother had a bad miscarriage in the Royal Infirmary in Aberdeen. It was a boy. She never told me it was a boy, it was my father who did. She then got some awful blood poisoning, the kind that sheep get through dirt. She was really very ill and the doctor told her not to try for another child for five years. Of course medicine was completely different in those days.

My parents moved back to Provender in 1949, by which time Mother was *just* pregnant with me. She was convinced I was a boy. Mother thought I was going to be 'The Prince', and I was practically put down for Eton and my life was all mapped out.

I was born by Caesarean section in the Welbeck Clinic in Queen's Gate, now long gone. When Mother came round from the anesthetic (I think it was some form of ether in 1950) and was told it was a girl, she burst into tears.

My father rang my grandfather Herbert McDougall and complained, "She doesn't like the baby. She doesn't want a girl," and Herbert said, "Don't worry Andrew; it'll be fine when she wakes up properly." And it was.

I was born in April 1950 and I was brought down to Provender when I was two weeks old. My father already had three children by his first marriage; one was twenty-nine and the other two were in their thirties when I was born. They thought of me as a spoilt brat. Not that I had jewels or lots of money thrown at me. That would have been quite nice. No, it was a *different* kind of spoiling. My mother was so old for the time. She was two months short of her forty-second birthday, and Pa was fifty-four, so they didn't try for another baby. I think I was enough really!

3

NURSERY DAYS

I WAS CHRISTENED on 16 May 1950 in the Orthodox chapel at
Wilderness House, Hampton Court, one of the grace and favour
homes of my grandmother Xenia. According to *The Times,* my
christening dress was made from lace which had belonged to my great-
grandmother Dagmar, the exiled Empress Maria Feodorovna.

My mother was so nervous that her precious child would drown in
the baptismal font that she bought a shallow baby's bath to put inside
it, so that I couldn't be dunked fully in the water as is customary in
the Orthodox Church. I believe I cried at one point which is good,
because they say if you cry it lets the devil out of you.

The same newspaper also listed my godparents as King Haakon of
Norway, Queen Ingrid of Denmark, my grandmother Grand Duchess
Xenia, my uncle Prince Rostislav, my grandfather Colonel Herbert
McDougall, Mrs Carlos Fountaine of Narford Hall in Norfolk and
Mrs George Wheler.

In the Orthodox Church the godparents are family members. In the
Church of England it's different, as the parents choose people who are
not necessarily members of the family. My parents were very short
sighted in this matter because you should always get godparents *younger*
than yourselves. They chose godparents who were older than them.

My godparents all gave me nice Christening presents though. King
Haakon gave a brooch and Queen Ingrid's present was a bracelet.
My mother put them in the bank.

By the time I was born, parents generally *did* interact more with their
children than they had before the war – fathers now were prepared to

push the baby's pram, although my father had done this also for his other children.

But my pram was something special. My mother wanted only the very best. Just before I was born, she approached the Queen's coach builders and asked them to make her the same pram as they had made for Prince Charles. So I had an identical pram which was ready for me when I was brought down to Provender. It had a removable loose floor, so that you could sit with your feet in the well when you got past the stage of lying in it, and you could, in theory, put one child at either end. Later when I used the pram for my own son in 1976 or '77, it was *brilliant* for pinching vegetables or fruit from the farm – with my baby son lying on the mattress, the hollow bit underneath was completely concealed!

But back to my time in the pram. Pa would take me for a walk to the farm, which was part of our estate, when I was around two, three or four. Because I was quite lazy, I would usually stay in the pram. Pa didn't want me to get a draught, and when it was windy, he would put the hood up and I would scream "No, no, Papa! Down, down!"

It would go up, I'd put it down – and it went on and on, much to the amusement of the men working in the big fruit trees nearby. They enjoyed coming to watch the tussle between the prince and his little girl.

We've still got that pram but it's almost completely collapsed now and not much use for smuggling fruit.

My mother had a monthly nurse who came to Provender with her when I was born. Sister Helen Rowe, known as Rowey, attended the births of all the Queen's children. She looked after Prince Charles, Princess Anne and possibly also Prince Andrew and Prince Edward. Wanting only the best, Mother presumed the Queen only *had* the best.

The nursery wing was on the second floor of the house. My grandmother converted the best guestroom into the most *amazing* nursery. It also had a nursery bathroom, nursery corridor and a night nursery, all overseen by a nanny, an *under* nanny and a nursery maid. Can you imagine? All these people to look after *one* child! And although they weren't there all at the same time, it was my own warm, cosy little world.

The nursery wing had a special cork floor so that it was easy for the nursery maid to scrub. I can remember sitting on my pot in front of the electric fire (it couldn't be a real fire because my mother was worried I might get burnt) watching the poor old maid on her hands and knees with a scrubbing brush, a block of Fairy soap and a *huge* bucket, scrubbing away.

These buckets were quite high. One day, when I was toddling around, my ear caught in the handle and the rim of the bucket cut my ear very badly. That was the end of the buckets. Mother got some other kind of device for the water after that.

I was a *very* precious child. I wasn't allowed to drink tap water, I had only Malvern water. The milkman wasn't allowed to call during the polio season, because Mother thought the wheels could pick up germs like foot and mouth. – in fact that's proved to be correct. There are a lot of things my mother said were bad which have since turned out to be correct.

Mother had a thing about being germ free. When people came to visit and wanted to see the precious baby, she would say, "Do you have a cold, are you germy?" In those days there was something called 'Flit' which came in a canister. You pumped it up and sprayed it all over the room. Of course it was DDT, but nobody knew then that DDT was poisonous.

So before visitors were allowed to go and look at the darling baby in the nursery, she sprayed them with this DDT, rather like they used to do years ago when you got off an aeroplane.

The nursery later became my bedroom. It was perfectly normal. The nursery was where children slept and I liked being there.

When I was about six months old my grandmother Xenia came to stay for a long weekend. To me she was 'Amama', the endearment used by the Danish Royal family for 'Grandmother' ('Apapa' was Grandfather). Amama enjoyed her stay at Provender. She was given the best guest room, she went out and met people and my parents gave a party for her. She got on well with my grandmother Sylvia too. They spent a lot of time talking together, although apparently in typical fashion Sylvia was inclined to pile on the use of Amama's title – saying 'Grand Duchess' this or that every two minutes.

Another visitor was Aunt Titti, my father's only sister, who married Felix Yusupov, one of Rasputin's murderers. They used to visit England from their base in Paris and we'd see her every now and again because she'd go through Kent on her way to Hampton Court to see her mother.

I don't know why she was called Titti, but I remember her so well because she also could do caricatures and funny drawings. When I was little she used to come in when I was sitting on my pot and draw little caricatures of animals sitting on pots. I was very fond of her. She smelt of *Gauloise* cigarettes and Chanel No. 5. Her voice was very deep and she spoke many languages. She was terribly funny and *wonderful* with small children.

When I was really young, Mother would stay in bed until eleven o'clock and there were times when she expected the nursery governess or the nanny to bring me into her room so I could say good morning.

One morning we forgot to do that. Mother was absolutely furious with the poor woman for not bringing the child in to say good morning to her mother. That was one of her snobbish ideas that didn't last long!

When Papa would say goodnight to me he would always kiss me three times on the cheeks, then kiss me on the palm of each hand and speak to me in Russian. When I visit Russia I recognise certain words that Pa used to say to me.

I wasn't taught Russian, unlike Pa's other children who spoke the language fluently.

I only speak English – and because I lived in Scotland for so many years, I come out with many Scottish idioms.

Pa also used to bath me when the nanny was off and if my mother was busy. I remember him saying that before the Stone Age, toes were like hands. So I'd lie in the bath and he'd say, "Open your toes. Make your toes stretch like your hands. Separate them." And I'd do it.

We had lots of nannies. I was only three months old when the first one came, so I don't remember her. I do remember though being pushed up the lane in my pushchair. We nicknamed this lane the 'poofy road'

because they were just doing the hop fields. It was the first time they'd grown hops and there were lots of piles of manure all around. You could see the steam rising from the ground and because my pushchair was quite low I remember the bad smell.

The first nannies I do remember were Nanny Ray and Nanny Eileen, who alternated with us for some time. If I became too fond of the nannies, they were sacked, except for Nanny Ray, who I adored and just wanted to hug.

Nanny Ray, the most *wonderful* woman on earth, came here in 1953. She lived at 99 Main Street, St Bees, Cumberland, which is now Cumbria. She must have been in her fifties when she came to us. She had grey hair and pulled it back with lots of Kirby grips. The elastic round her bloomers held up her Nora Batty-type stockings. They were thick stockings with a seam down the back and she'd pull them up and put the elastic of her bloomers over them to act as garters. She never wore a bra, so her boobs hung down, and she always wore Viyella shirts, a navy skirt, an apron and slip-on shoes. She didn't wear a uniform.

But Mother didn't want Nanny Ray to spend more than three months at a time here. So she'd come for three months then go on to other jobs, rotating families during the year. She stayed with us until 1966. She came to my wedding too. I put her up in the Dorchester with us and I remember her saying to me, "You will be kind to him, won't you."

When Nanny Ray wasn't here we often had Nanny Eileen, who had been at college with her. Nanny Eileen wore narrow striped pure cotton dresses in varying colours, which she washed in the bath because we didn't have the luxury of washing machines in those days. So when she put them in the water an air bubble appeared. It fascinated me to watch this air bubble get bigger and bigger as she pushed the dress further down into the water.

Nanny Eileen was a bit eccentric; she used to see fairies on the mantelpiece. But she did wonderful Teddy Bears' parties in the walled garden and in the field amongst the cherry trees. I had several teddy bears and they were all nearly as big as me. There was Sandy Bear and his brother Edward. Then I was given Caroline and then Ricky. He was very white and fluffy and it said on the bottom of his foot, "Please wash me in Persil". The moths got poor Ricky and he died a nasty death. So we had the Teddy Bears' Tea Party, the Teddy Bears' Wedding and the Teddy Bears' Christening. It was great fun. We used to have these picnics on cine film, but sadly the films have deteriorated and have gone blank. As I was an only child, these bears were my friends. Quite sad really.

Nanny Eileen also did wonderful flowers and decorations, especially at Christmas. Unfortunately Nanny Eileen was sacked. It was near Christmas and my grandmother wanted help upstairs in her own suite. So Mother called out, "My mother wants you, Nanny!"

But Nanny Eileen was busy with her decorations so she replied, "Oh well, she'll have to wait fifteen minutes, because I'm busy with this!" And that was it. She was sacked the next day. Mother liked *total* politeness from anyone who worked for her.

We had two Christmas celebrations, one on 25 December and then the Russian one on 7 January. That was lovely when I was a child because I also received two lots of presents. As my mother was of Finnish descent we had Christmas presents on Christmas Eve, so I wasn't allowed to see the tree until then. It was always an 8 foot tree at the bottom of the Oak Room and Father decorated it beautifully. In those days you could have little candle holders with *real* candles, and the tree never caught fire. It was so big and beautiful with all the coloured balls and long threads of shiny lametta dangling down. It was wonderful.

I was let into the Oak Room after tea on Christmas Eve. All the presents were laid out, Granny would come down from her suite and nanny would be there too. Then we had a big meal, usually a turkey. The next day there would be a cold meal, or a hot ham depending on who was coming to visit us.

We did the whole thing again for the Russian Christmas in January. There were not as many presents for the adults at the Russian Christmas. Both Christmas Days were treated the same, although perhaps on one we had a turkey and on the other a goose, depending on what Mother felt like. She used to enjoy cooking on important days such as Christmas.

My mother being Scandinavian, she would encourage me to drink champagne from about the age of six. "Have a sip darling, it's good luck." I got bolshie towards my teens and refused to drink it, but secretly I loved it.

As well as the nannies I also had nursery governesses, who came for a few hours every day. My parents employed the first one quite by accident. I think Pa must have been at Hampton Court looking after Amama, and Mother was having an operation in London for gall bladder. So I was left with this awful witch – a really *poisonous* nanny. She was the only nanny who wore a uniform and she was a real witch from hell.

I always had to have a rest in my room in the afternoon and during this period I sometimes wanted to go to the loo. But nanny wouldn't let me get up. She was *really* strict.

Years later, in 1976, I was looking for a good nanny for my first child. I wanted someone for a few months from the time the baby was born. So I rang the agency. After a few minutes chatting to me they said, "Oh we do have a very responsible lady. One of the best nannies on our books is Nanny —."

"No! "I said, at the mention of her name. "She was poison when I was little!"

Although I disliked her she was quite good as a nursery school teacher and she taught me to read at a very young age. By the time I was four or five I could read a book without a problem. I couldn't add up, but I *could* read and could just about write as well. First they taught you to do pages of 'a', then pages of 'b' and then at some point you actually put them together. I think she decided to teach me to keep me out of mischief!

In the summer we used to go to a beach at Seasalter, near Whitstable. It had shingle, then mud when the tide was out. I was about five years old and I was wading out into the sea behind my mother. When I came back to nanny my big toe was hanging off. I'd trodden on a bottle and it had cut right through to the bone.

Pa was always very calm in a crisis. Mother didn't believe in hysteria either, because she believed *our* class shouldn't show hysteria. I remember Mother was sitting in the back of Father's little car and he was driving, I was sitting on nanny's lap and she was pouring Malvern water over my toe to get the sand and the mud out.

We arrived at the Cottage Hospital and I was lying on the bed in the surgery. My mother put her finger in my mouth and said, "*We* do not cry or make a noise. Bite on this." I had six stitches in my big toe. I still can't bend it.

Nanny was with us for quite a long time because my parents actually liked her. Then she fell in love with the gardener's brother and that ruined it all. Nanny became less focused on her job and then left because Mother showed her annoyance.

After the ghastly nanny there was another governess Mother found in town called Miss Stein. She was a typical governess type of woman, small, thin, with grey hair in a bun and very sweet. She came with good credentials and she used to take me for long walks.

One day I went upstairs for my rest as usual and there was a commotion in the house. Miss Stein had suffered an epileptic fit at the top of the stairs. My mother was livid. She shouted at the doctor who had advised her to employ the woman – "How dare you not tell me! She could have had a fit while walking my precious child! The child wouldn't have known what to do and wouldn't know how to get back!" So the poor woman was asked to leave but Mother gave her a generous severance payment.

After Miss Stein we had a local nursery governess to teach me a bit more. She was lovely. Her name was Ann and she and her husband were potters. She'd arrived with a great lump of clay and all we seemed to do was play with her potter's clay and make things and kneed them as we chatted.

After Ann it was the turn of another local woman, a farmer's wife from Selling. She was my nursery governess until I was about nine. We did our lessons in the library, where I had a lovely desk with a huge toy sheep next to me.

I used to make her lift her skirt up at the side to show me the underpants she was wearing. One day, when I was about six, Mother caught me asking her to do this and show Papa her coloured pants. Mother soon put a stop to that. She said it was totally unsuitable to get the governess to lift her skirt in front of my father.

Every day I had to write to Amama at Hampton Court. It was

always the same dreadfully dull kind of letter: "Darling Amama, today I ..." Then I told her what I was doing, and usually ended with: "I hope you are feeling better. With all my love, Olga."

Amama loved art and was very good at it, so I always enclosed a drawing with my letter. We cheated though – my governess did the drawing, I only coloured it in!

Sometimes we had visits from my Romanov uncles. My father had five brothers, Some of them lived in England and at least three stayed in England a *lot* but also travelled a lot. One lived and died in the UK but he also had a house in France.

Uncle Vassili, Pa's youngest brother, stayed in England for a while when Amama was ill then eventually moved back to the States. His wife was Princess Natalia Galitzine, who he met when she was playing small parts in Hollywood films. But Vassili was quite poor. Everybody looked after him because they all adored him and his wife, so they lived in grace-and-favour-type places. At one time he ran a chicken farm in California.

Vassili was very naughty and had a great sense of humour. His party trick was to stand on his head and balance an empty champagne bottle on his nose. He was by far the funniest of my father's brothers.

Marina, Uncle Vassili's daughter, was wonderful. I haven't seen her since 1965 but I do speak to her occasionally and I'm friends with her children. In the sixties Marina and Billy, whom she later married, were doing a grand tour of Europe in a mini van. They pitched up at Provender unannounced one summer and my mother of course told her, "Do come and stay the night." But, she added – in a typical double standard because she was worried about morals – "You can't possibly share a room because of the child." She didn't want *me* to see an unmarried couple sharing a room.

One of my other uncles stayed in the servants' wing at Provender during the 1950s. I think it was Rostislav. There were no live-in staff then, so he was there for quite a while.

He was an alcoholic, so every day he used to take a taxi to a really low dive of a pub in Faversham called 'The Hole in the Wall' and spend all day there until he was so drunk that he fell off the bar stool. Then he'd get into a taxi and come home again. He did that for quite a long time but apparently everybody adored him, he was really good fun. When he got to the pub they'd just say, "Here comes the Prince.'

Mother didn't mind either. Men can get away with an awful lot more than women. He occupied a different wing of the house which had its own front door. He was also very funny, so he sang for his supper. I don't know what happened to him after that. I think he pulled himself together and married again.

My uncle on my mother's side, her brother-in-law George Sondes, had terrible DTs (delirium tremens), caused by alcohol. He used to call the police out all the time, because he was convinced 'those black people' were digging a grave for him at the bottom of his garden at Lees Court. "Oh yes, my Lord, yes My Lord," the police would say. So they'd come out and look. "Oh, I can't find them, my Lord..." And off they would go.

About every ten days we would go to Wilderness House to visit Amama. I used to take Communion with her Father Confessor, a wonderful man called Father George Cheremetiev. After the service we always had a big lunch in the dining room.

When Amama died Father Cheremetiev became my priest.

There was also a tradition that everyone etched their name on an upstairs window, but I wasn't allowed to do it as I was only a child.

To get to Amama you had to get past Mother Martha. She was quite scary, although she didn't mind the family. I know very little about her because Amama died in 1960 when I was ten but, according to my cousin Alexander, Uncle Nikita's younger son, her real name was Vera Maslenikoff and she was a nun and a nurse. I believe she helped in the Crimea.

Father told my mother that one day, back in the Crimea, Mother Martha had gone down the ward to inspect the beds. Everything would look clean, and all the patients had a white sheet up to their chin. Then she'd rip the white sheet back, only to find that they were covered in maggots and gangrene. All that cleanliness was just a sham.

Mother Martha was a very tall woman and a stickler for how things should be done. She obviously adored Amama. She wore a white wimple that just showed her face which was completely framed in white with a starched veil that came below her shoulders. She wore a black robe.

When I was around four or five I was quite fond of her and used to sit on her knee. But as I grew older I found her creepy and she couldn't understand why I was no longer willing to be sweet to her.

I adored Amama. She was lovely and had a great sense of humour. She had a Fabergé cigarette holder and there was a bowl, like a stone dog's bowl at her feet, and it had fag ends swimming in it. I always thought it was rather disgusting because I didn't know it wasn't a dog's bowl, it looked like dog poo to me.

This was before the days of filter cigarettes, so she'd cut her cigarette into three, and put a piece into the cigarette holder and smoke a bit. As she didn't like the smell of fag ends around, she would take it out and throw it in the water bowl. Then Mother Martha would come along and empty the bowl. It was strange. Amama was very jolly and I've got lots of photographs of us together in the garden.

In her later years Amama would be lying in bed when we visited. At that time I used to ride my pony a lot and for some reason she was fascinated by my thighs, which were muscular. Mother would dress me in these vile dresses with smocking. I wanted to be in my jeans but obviously I wasn't allowed to. So I'd have to lift up my dress so Amama could poke her finger into my thigh to feel the muscles.

Mother Martha had her favourites, one of whom was my cousin Alexander, I believe. After Amama died Mother Martha would just hand these favourites a little box – "Here you are dear," – and it would be a little bit of Fabergé, so rumour has it. Alexander had always been very nice to Mother Martha.

There were nurses to look after Amama towards the end but Mother Martha was very jealous and resented them. She liked to be completely in control of Amama. I don't know what happened to her after Amama died, nobody seems to know. When everybody came out of the church after the funeral she had disappeared. It was a total mystery.

Alexander was also very fond of my mother and used to stay with us for weekends after Amama's death. His great friend was Paul Getty, who although worth billions was very mean. Alexander often stayed at Sutton Place and Paul Getty had guard dogs roaming the corridors so that none of the guests could get out of their rooms to go and get a drink. Alexander was very fond of whisky, so he was seriously annoyed that after lights out he couldn't get a dram to take back to his bedroom. There were even pay phones installed for guests to use. So when Getty had gone out Alexander would go into *his* room and use the telephone by his bed. Getty was surprisingly careful with his money.

In the 1960s there was a lot of talk about Anna Anderson, who claimed to be the Tsar's daughter Anastasia, saved from the Ekaterinburg massacre. Pa spoke about it a lot. He said she was a batty woman and nothing to do with us. She was a fraud.

Alexander went to visit her and just knew she wasn't right. All the Romanovs had their teeth and ear prints taken and none of these matched hers. But most importantly, I remember Alexander saying that she wasn't beautiful and she didn't speak Russian. Papa thought it was a stunt to obtain the Tsar's money and she obviously believed there *was* money involved – and of course there wasn't. Nicholas had ordered that their money be brought back to Russia from European banks at the start of the First World War.

I was still a child then and the Anastasia business didn't bother me one way or the other. My chief love in life was ponies and horses.

I first sat on a pony at the Tickham Hunt Meet when I was three. Mother used to have ponies 'on trial' because she was very worried about her one and only child, so if the ponies kicked, bucked or gave any trouble they were usually sent back. I wouldn't even know about it until the next day.

The exception was a lovely little Shetland pony called Linda, which looked like a Thelwell pony – you couldn't tell which way she was going, she was identical back and front. Linda was with us for a long time, then she got laminitis and had to be put down. I saw her being put down and carted off upside down to the kennels to be eaten by the hounds. But I was a robust child.

I remember one hilarious occasion when Linda came into the house. Mother gave what she called 'Hen's Lunches' for ladies only, mainly her friends and the local great and the good. I was too young to attend, I was only about five, but I was allowed to come down and see them when they had coffee.

In those days women wore hats for lunch and some of them were quite elaborate. One of the guests was a lovely woman called Lady Harris, the daughter-in-law of the great cricketer who lived at Belmont Park near Faversham. During lunch Linda was brought into the house by the old gardener. She came down the steps to the Oak Room and walked round the guests at the table. Dolly Harris was wearing a hat decorated with lots of spring flowers – and the pony made a lurch for the flowers and grabbed at her hat. Dolly was horrified.

We had lots of animals at Provender. When I was little there were about five fighting cocks with two-inch spurs, which were bred along with our farmyard cocks and about thirty hens. Before the war my mother had bred fighting cocks. I don't think she used them to fight but she liked the strain because they bred well, the eggs were good and the flesh was delicious to eat.

At the back of the house we had a large breeding dog kennel, built on two floors with a concrete piece in front and mesh around it. In fact it was so big that I was able to take the furniture from the Wendy House and put it in there. Then I began training these huge birds to sit on the chairs and eat corn out of the dolls' cups. And they did it! I was only tiny and these huge birds were so sweet with me.

I also had a pet hen called Suzanna. Every afternoon the nursery governess took me for a walk on the farm. So I wrapped Suzanna in a shawl, put her in the dolls' pram and took her with me. She never failed to lay an egg for me every day.

Then one Sunday the gardener was sent to kill a chicken for lunch. We ate the chicken and I thought no more of it – until afterwards, when I went out to search for Suzanna she wasn't there. So I said to the gardener: "Mr Moss, which bird did you kill?" And it turned out that he'd wrung Suzanna's neck and I'd eaten her.

Luckily, as I said, I was a robust child. If you live in the country-side you can't be too feeble, you just accept these things as a fact of life.

Mother wanted goats because she thought they would eat the weeds and be generally helpful. She hired a big chauffeur driven limo and we went off to see a very eccentric woman who lived in the middle of the forest with lots of goats. We chose a mother, nanny and its kid, a random one that was a young teenager and another kid that had just been weaned. They all came back to Provender in the back of the car.

Goats produce pellets *ad nauseam* but Mother had absolutely no idea where she was going to put these animals. We got them into the house and they ran amok, up and down the stairs, dropping these pellets as they went. She got rid of them the next day.

Pa had geese in the front field and they were wonderful as burglar alarms. One particularly huge gander was nearly as tall as me when its head was up. One day it went for me. I was wearing a dress, probably one of the reasons I hate dresses now, and it went for my bottom, got hold of the cheek and pinched it and turned at the same time. It was very painful. I squealed like a pig and had a big bruise.

Pa always looked after the chicks and the goslings. We hatched them ourselves in special runs and he was very good at looking after them when they were little. He was extremely patient with animals and children and incredibly good as a parent. We'd go off into the woods and he would build beautiful little houses out of twigs and sticks. Then he would make a whole little village of these houses for me to look at and play with. Sometimes we'd make mud pies and come back and bake them in the Aga.

He carved all the furniture for my dolls' house too. It was wasted though, as I absolutely loathed dolls. I liked guns, the soldiers in my fort and farms. I was a complete tomboy.

Long before I was born he also did little carvings. They looked like fire screens – but when the screen was taken up, there was the whole *Kama Sutra*. But that was Pa. He had a *different* sense of humour.

Father was very hands on as far as I was concerned, which I think slightly upset my half siblings because he hadn't been like that with them. The life they led with Pa and his first wife, was completely different, because he'd been so busy and the children were left with their nannies to be looked after. In those days parents didn't spend time in the nursery or playing with the children. It wasn't the done thing; whereas he was with me 24/7 for part of my childhood.

My father indulged me but my mother was *very* strict. She smacked me on the bottom if I was bad. My father never ever smacked me. I could tell when he was angry, his voice would change and he'd shrug his shoulders and glare, but there was no aggression of any sort.

My parents were old, so I was brought up with old people. Granny was in her eighties when I was born and it didn't seem strange to me. I didn't compare it to my friends.

When we went to London Mother was frightfully grand. She was quite scary, because if I didn't toe the line I got the icy blue eyes.

My parents and I would often go to have lunch or tea at the Ritz. The Palm Room at the Ritz was *the* place to have tea in those days. It was immaculate before they crammed in all the extra tables for tourists. There were fish in the golden bowl of the fountain and I used to bend over with my bottom in the air, trying to catch them. One day the wonderful *maître d'* said to my mother, "Aren't you going to get her a fishing licence?"

Nanny always came with us. One day I was restless – I suppose there must have been some boring people around – so she was told to take me to the cloakroom so I could let off steam. The Ladies' room had a very large sofa, so nanny sat on it. I was bored, so kept bouncing on the sofa – and I broke the springs.

Mother always liked to be in the forefront, so she would say to us, "You walk three paces behind me." She said this to my *father* too – and my father was the prince!

When I was a child we would always go to Harrods and Fortnum & Mason but I had to know my place. Fortnum's was beautiful then, absolutely stunning, and the toy department was better than Harrods, so we'd always go and have a look. And if by chance I tried to run ahead, Mother's arm would come across and stop me. "Walk behind me!" She could be really difficult. But when I grew up and came into my teens it wasn't so bad. At home she was also more relaxed.

When I was about nine, Mother thought that perhaps they'd send me to the local Catholic Convent in Sittingbourne as a day pupil. Lots of the girls around the area went there so she thought it would be a good idea.

The nuns saw my exercise books and everything was fine. Or so my mother thought.

I turned up for the first day in this *hideous* turd-brown uniform with a hat that was pulled down like a pot. It had a yellow logo on it and the uniform was completed with a tunic and a Viyella shirt underneath, white socks up to the knee, ugly brown sandals, a satchel and a brown blazer. My mother picked me up after my first day and said I looked like a squashed cowpat.

On the first day I went to my classroom where the nun in charge looked at my books and began asking me questions. She thought I was *really* thick. So instead of placing me facing her alongside the rest of the class, my desk was moved to *face* the class!

It turned out the nursery governess had cooked the books. She'd made me *look* clever, but she'd been doing everything for me and she hadn't actually taught me anything.

I didn't know what bullying was. I remember standing in the playground and being surrounded by a group of slightly older children who were jeering at me and saying things such as "What's it like being a princess?" They were really mean, but I hadn't a clue what they were talking about having led such a sheltered life. I still didn't quite twig that this isn't what you should do to people.

Then I got whooping cough. My mother hadn't allowed me to have any of the childhood diseases. I wasn't allowed near people with any kind of illness because of her worry about germs. Worse still, I passed the whooping cough on to her. She was so ill poor woman! We both were. Luckily I recovered quite quickly.

I did three, maybe four weeks at the beginning of the school's summer term before I was sick. Then everyone realized that it was a *huge* mistake to have sent me there.

So I never went back to school.

4

WILD IN KENT

AFTER THE DISASTROUS experiment with school my parents had to find me a governess who could actually *teach* me. We had some friends a few miles away who had a very clever daughter called Yvonne. She had been attending school but her parents decided that they wanted her educated at home. Her governess, a wonderful woman called Mrs Ebbutt, had been a school teacher and Mother persuaded her, poor thing, to come and teach me as well. She taught me from when I was nine until I was sixteen.

Our day was structured just like any school day. Mrs Ebbutt arrived at twenty to nine; we'd start on the *dot* of nine o'clock and have a break at eleven for fifteen minutes. At half past twelve we went down to the kitchen for lunch, then lessons continued from half-past one until half-past three.

We followed a curriculum set by the Parents' National Educational Union, the P.N.E.U. I don't think they're in existence any longer but they were around for quite a long time.

The P.N.E.U. was started for ex-pats, such as the tea planters in India or the coffee planters in Africa, to educate their children before they sent little Freddy or little Johnny back to boarding school in England at about the age of twelve. The P.N.E.U. set the coursework and the private tutor or the governess had to follow it. At the end of each term they sent out a list of books so you could order them in time for the start of the next term and follow the curriculum. Everything was set. Their emblem was a flying swallow and it appeared on all their exercise books and text books.

At the end of the summer term I had to take exams. The questions were again set by the P.N.E.U., who also set the time limit for the examination. Mrs Ebbutt would say "You've got half an hour to do this," or maybe it was an hour, then she'd give me the A4 paper and leave the room. But as my only interest was ponies and horses, that's what I wrote about mainly.

Unfortunately, my mother checked the paper before it was sent off to London. She made me rewrite my composition, because she wasn't keen about me talking about nothing but ponies. She thought it was too much for the examiners to see that this was my *only* interest.

Mother also disliked my style of handwriting. I had been taught to write in quite a flowery way, with lots of unnecessary loops and curls. For instance, the 'M's had lots of loops, the 'F's were back-to-front, and the letters 'Y' and 'G' also had each a big loop.

When my mother was checking my work she said to Mrs Ebbutt: "This is hideous. This is common, this is ghastly. Teach her to write properly." So, at the age of about ten I had to *totally* relearn to write in the way that Mother thought was acceptable. That must be why I have such terrible handwriting now.

Mrs Ebbutt spoke fluent French but she had a hard job teaching me the language. My French was *appalling*, and my interest even smaller. I regret that now, of course. It was all quite hard work.

Papa spoke five languages – Russian, Italian, French, English and German – but somebody once said they were all spoken very badly. That wasn't quite true. He *did* speak good English but because he spoke all those languages with a very strong foreign accent apparently all the languages came out sounding the same. All the family had this particular way of speaking. It was said that the Romanov men spoke five languages but said nothing in any of them!

When Aunt Titti and the uncles came to Provender they spoke only in Russian to each other. They wrote letters to each other in Russian too. My mother didn't speak Russian, nor did I, so we would just sit and listen. That was fine, we were used to it. Amama spoke English if other people were present, she was far too polite to speak a language that nobody else understood. But if they were together just *en famille*, they would speak Russian. Otherwise Pa spoke English with Mother and me but he said he always dreamt in Russian.

One day when Aunt Titti was visiting we went to see some friends who had a lovely estate called Torry Hill. There was a beautiful small gauge railway track that ran all around the estate and it had a real little steam engine. We all went on the railway, through the tunnels and back to the station. Somebody asked her, "Was that really nice Princess?"

"No," Aunt Titti replied, "I've got soot in my eye." It was really painful, and she had to go to the Cottage Hospital to have the soot removed.

Although I was fond of Aunt Titti, I was never allowed to meet her husband Prince Felix Yusupov. Pa had never forgiven him for his part in Rasputin's murder.

In his youth Felix had been well-known as a transvestite. Once he dressed in women's clothes and went with his brother to the Paris Opéra. He looked so convincing that he attracted the admiring eye of King Edward VII. When the King asked for an introduction to the 'lovely young woman', Felix and his brother had to beat a hasty retreat.

Felix then took a job as a nightclub singer, again wearing women's clothes. His potential career ended abruptly when some of his mother's friends recognised the family jewels he was wearing. The resulting scandal had to be hushed up.

It was a well-known fact that when Felix was older he liked to wear thick make-up all over his face. I think it was called Pan make-up, made by Max Factor and came on a stick. I used to buy it when I was about fourteen and my mother was absolutely horrified.

The first time my mother met Felix, she decided to play a little trick on him. They all happened to be at the Ritz at the same time, so first of all Mother went to the Ladies' room and put on thick, red lipstick in a cupid bow on her lips. And when she was introduced to Felix she kissed him on both cheeks. Everybody kissed each other, it was a sort of foreign thing. So there was a big bow of a kiss on one cheek and then she planted another on the other cheek. Poor old Felix had to go off to the Gents' and spend a lot of time wiping off *his* make-up and *her* lipstick! He didn't like my mother.

Many years later I stayed with Aunt Titti's and Felix's daughter 'Baby' Cheremetiev in Athens. She was absolutely divine. I also met her daughter, Xenia, known as 'Puntka'. She and her husband Ilya were also staying in the house. It was a really hot day in August and I was lying in my bikini in the garden. Out rushed Puntka. "No, no, you can't lie like that. Ilya might see you!" she shouted angrily. So she made me get dressed and took me to church.

The best-looking of my five Romanov uncles was Feodor, who lived in France and died there of TB in 1968. He was married and had a son, Michel, who lived in Paris and who has now also died. For some reason I never met Feodor.

I only met Michel once. He was in the film industry for many years and one of the productions he worked on was the Ingrid Bergman and Yul Brynner film *Anastasia*. Michel was asked to take photographs of Amama's rooms at Wilderness House, so that they could recreate the atmosphere of the Dowager Empress's rooms when she lived in exile at Hvidøre in Denmark.

Uncle Dmitri lived in Belgravia with his second wife Sheila. It was one of those elegant tall houses with four floors and a kitchen in the basement. They had a pet white rabbit, which was house trained and used to sleep behind the Aga in the kitchen. On each floor around the house they had boxes, like cat litter trays, so he could go and do his business. It was so sweet.

They and their friends were all heavy drinkers. So when Dmitri gave grand lunches or dinners the guests would come rolling out of the dining room and see a white rabbit climbing the stairs in front of them – they all thought they had the DTs! But this rabbit was amazing.

All the uncles had children, but none of them lived in Britain. As soon as they were old enough they all emigrated to Canada and America, the *mecca* of all things good in those days.

Mother wanted to keep me at home because I could be educated better and be moulded better. One of her favourite sayings was: "Give me the child for the first seven years and I will mould its character."

I had been taught to ride by the father of my friend Yvonne, so Mother bought a couple of Irish donkeys because she thought they would be safer than ponies. My best friend Vicky, who lived up the road, had a big brown Spanish donkey called Dolores. I had Bambino and Gill. Gill always came with us too because she had no bridle and she used to follow the others. Although people say donkeys are stubborn, these animals went really fast and could jump bales of hay and straw without any problem, so we used to have Donkey Derbys. My friend's gardener built Grand National type fences for us, although they were only just over a foot high. So we'd gallop down the straight and go over the jumps on the donkeys.

We set up a little circus as well. We rode the donkeys bareback, either with a halter or a bridle without a noseband. There was no saddle. So we leapfrogged onto the back of our animals, then stood on their backs barefoot and did circus tricks with them. It was all great fun. Occasionally we'd invite my mother to watch, but she'd say, "*Ohhhhh, that's too dangerous!*"

My mother used to say to Vicky's mother, "Oh, my one and only!" and Mary, Vicky's mother, would say to me, "Does your mother think because she's got one child and I've got four, that I love any of them less?"

Although Mother was very protective and didn't let me have any freedom, I was occasionally allowed to go to Vicky's house for the day and as a treat she'd let me stay the night. I used to *love* that. I was never homesick. I sometimes had friends staying at Provender for weekends during the summer holidays as well.

When I was younger, one of Vicky's brothers used the word fart. I'd never heard the word before because I was so protected, so I used this word and Mother was furious. She rang up poor Mary and said "How dare Simon use words like that in front of my daughter!"

Mother was always very worried about me and I suppose in some ways I *was* rather accident prone. One day Vicky and I had been playing with a really thick rope. We hung it between two trees in the wild bit of the field and then we rode the donkeys bareback as usual. One donkey followed the other, so Vicky went through with Delores and I was on another donkey. As we cantered through the trees the rope caught me and took me off the back of the donkey by my neck. It left two huge rope burns, just as if I'd been strangled.

I knew my mother would go ballistic when I got home so, although it was quite warm weather, I borrowed a polo neck sweater and pulled it up so the rope burns didn't show. But by now it was beginning to hurt quite a bit.

Later that evening my mother picked me up. When we got back to the house she said, "Why are you wearing that sweater?" It was a warm evening and I must have looked guilty, so Mother moved the polo neck down, saw the rope burns and she freaked.

She got the doctor to come out immediately to check for any kind of bacteria and to see whether I'd done any damage to my neck. She was afraid that all her plans for a 'brilliant marriage' for me would go down the tube because I was going to have scars round my neck.

It turned out to be fine but I wasn't allowed to go and play with Vicky for a few days. That was always my punishment. If I did something naughty or displeased Mother, she'd stop me going to play with Vicky.

Vicky's family had four domestic cats. Sometime later there was also a wild cat in one of their numerous sheds and garages. We could only see it through the cracks so I tried to entice it out. I put my arm in to grab it and it scratched me from elbow to wrist – but it was not just a scratch, it took huge gouges out of my arm. Again, I said nothing when I went back into the house.

Vicky's family had a nanny. So I went and found her and said, "Nanny, what do I do?" She disinfected my arm and dressed it for me but the wound was big, it was quite sore and by the time I got home it was throbbing. I couldn't cover it up and, once again, when my mother saw it she went ballistic.

After the donkeys I was allowed to have a pony again. The saddles in those days were really seriously uncomfortable, they had no knee rolls and weren't built like they are now. It was very flat where your knees went and with no padding, it was just straight down. My riding instructor would put a 10 shilling note between my right knee and the saddle, so that when I was trotting my knee went on the saddle. It makes you get the pressure right on the horse.

The whole balance of how you ride now has completely changed. In those days you rode long, and it was all quite uncomfortable. I do like riding short though, particularly when jumping and galloping.

I didn't do any circus tricks on the pony like I did on the donkey. I used to ride barefoot, but couldn't do that when I was having riding lessons because it was frowned upon by my instructor. Also I wasn't allowed to do anything hazardous. I didn't have jumping lessons, couldn't take part in the pony club, or go hunting. Mother said it was all far too risky and I resented that. My riding lessons never went beyond a fast trot because she would rush outside and say "Too fast! Too fast!"

Of course I liked a bit of an adrenaline rush, and as I couldn't have jumping lessons, I learnt from my friends when I rode with them. I jumped *really* high things like five-bar gates without any lessons and somehow I managed to stay on the horse. It was quite a big horse too. I don't know what my riding style must have been like.

The horses, donkeys and ponies all came into the house at various times and I used to ride them inside as well. In those days the postman actually came into the house to bring in the mail and take it away. I used to see him coming up the drive and when he came through the front door, I would go trotting towards him from the inside. It used to give him such a shock.

When I got bored with my lessons I'd say to Mrs Ebbutt, "I've got terrible tummy-ache – I'm going to the loo." I'd make sure I was there for at *least* half an hour, then I'd go out to the back of the house, catch my horse and go for a gallop. When I came back I would say in a feeble voice: "I'm feeling a little better now." The poor woman *must* have known what I was up to, but she never complained.

One day I took my horse over a really big jump on hard ground and he injured his leg. I don't know what I did to him exactly but I still feel guilty about it. Mother sold him back to where she bought him. After that I gave up riding... but only for a few months.

Mother hadn't ridden since she was young but she had a photograph taken of herself in riding kit on a friend's big grey horse. I think she thought she was going to ride again. She actually went to Lock's in London for her bowler hat, had handmade hunting boots and breeches (in those days they had little buttons below the knee, with little hooks to do them up). I presume she thought she might use them one day, but she would never have hunted because she didn't have the guts to do it. I think she went up the farm track a couple of times, posed for the photographs on the horse with me on a little pony – and that was it. The riding gear all went into the cupboard and she never wore it again. The boots are still in the hall at Provender with their wonderful trees inside. She spent a fortune – handmade hunting boots in 1957 were about £400 then, but they are beautifully made.

I remember Pa riding one of my ponies back home one day. It was quite a funny sight as it was only about 13.2 hands. Mother and I were following behind, and we could see Pa's legs almost touching the ground because he was so tall. The Romanov men were all quite tall.

He had a three-wheeled tractor, a Gunsmith, which I suppose they must have got after the war. It was a heavy piece of kit with a trailer, a plough and all sorts of other things. Pa was very keen on it. He often hitched the trailer to it and took me and my friends for rides around the farm which supplied the house.

We'd bounce around on the trailer, which didn't actually go very fast – this was long before ''elf and safety' became the bane of people's lives – and it was such fun! He was a good sport. The Gunsmith is still rotting in the garage, there's no roof on the building now.

When my friends were twelve they all went off to boarding schools like Bedgebury, Benendon and Lillesdon. I wanted to go too. My father's other children had gone to boarding school in this country, so it seemed the natural thing to do. But Mother had bad memories of her own time at boarding school.

At the age of eight she had been sent to a Tom Brown type-school. The teachers were *really cruel* and even at that young age she was made to carry heavy buckets. When the children went upstairs they weren't allowed to touch the banisters because they had been polished. They had to walk up the middle of the staircase. The dormitories didn't have heating. The place was so cold that Mother had *terrible* chill blains on her toes and fingers, which had to be bound in rags. So every night in bed the children would put their knees up as far as they could to their stomachs and put their hands between their legs to warm them. Then the old matron would come along and whip the bedclothes off, because she thought they might be playing with themselves. It was so awful that Mother swore that if she ever had a child, she wouldn't send it through that hell.

Actually she didn't realise that things had come on leaps and bounds since then and boarding school wasn't really the torture hole it had been for her. She always thought she was doing me a favour by leaving me at home with my governess. Pa left my upbringing to Mother, because he thought she knew best. He didn't realise that she hadn't got a clue. And because he was educated in the palace, and his cousins the Tsar's children had been brought up the same way, I don't think it struck him as odd that I was educated by governesses. He was *so* laid back, *so* easy going.

Stuck at home, I became a member of a gang with the farm boys. They weren't approved, of course. Mother had been horrified when at about the age of seven I came home with questions like, "What is it they stick inside you?" because I'd been given little bits of information by one of the farm boys. We used to play by the pond and try to make rafts and little boats.

As I got older, I became friendly with a different bunch of farm boys. We used to take tractors from the tractor shed and do burn ups on the farm, and would take out old lorries for a drive. The boys weren't just the locals, they came from miles around to be part of the gang. Their parents were all friends, so the boys would be dropped off to spend the day with little Freddy or whoever. We got into *huge* trouble though.

As the only girl I was the leader of the pack. It was really great. Nobody knew about my involvement. Mother didn't find out until the police came.

We'd been doing burn-ups on the tractors as usual. Now the tractor shed had a concertina door and that particular day the plough was sticking out. So as we went in, it literally went brrrrrr right the way round and ripped the door off. I took the can for that. In fact I took the can for everything, because I didn't want my friends to get into trouble.

My mother had flu and she was lying in bed when the big burly policeman, the local Constable Plod, went up to her room and told her. She was *mortified*. "Why are you saying you did this?" she asked me.

"Because it's true. I did."

There was a *frightful* rumpus. Mother had to pay for the door.

I'm still friends with the man whose farm it was back then. He remembers me and my little friends, girls this time, playing with the bushel boxes that held the apples. In those days the apples weren't in the huge bins they have now, so there was a huge stack of boxes in threes, one in the middle and two each side and we used to build a house inside, like a castle.

We did the same with straw bales, which was better as they didn't usually fall over. The straw was put there to use as insulation for the fruit trees. So we would build the castle before they could use the straw and of course it ruined it because the rain got in.

Looking back now, that was really dangerous. If straw bales collapse on you you're dead. It was huge fun though.

I suppose I was quite lonely and dysfunctional but one didn't really realise these things then. When I was about sixteen I used to tell Mother "It's a bloody good thing I'm not a boy because I would've been so gay." It was one of our arguments. She didn't like that. Maybe she wouldn't have cosseted me so much and would have allowed me more freedom if I had been a boy.

From about 1960, when I was ten, I was allowed to have dancing classes with friends. A man called Mr Wall who always came in a suit, was our dance teacher, I suppose he was the equivalent of one of the dance professionals on *Strictly*. He and his wife did exhibition dances at various places, where his wife would wear dresses that looked as if she had a meringue stuck on her bottom.

We had lessons in the hall once a week. I remember *Hello Mary Lou* with Ricky Nelson, which we jived to. I was useless at Rock 'n' Roll, but we also learnt the waltz, quick-step and cha-cha.

I also had ballet lessons in the drawing room. Mother said that my legs were totally bandy from the knees down because I had spent too much time on a pony as a little girl. This wasn't good for the marriage market.

The best way to straighten legs was to do ballet, because you stretched your legs and pointed your toes. So I had a ballet teacher for a few years and my legs went completely straight. Luckily, in those days they liked dancers to be quite short. And by the time I got to twelve

I was way taller than the teacher, so I had to give it up. Oh joy – because I *hated* it! I bracketed it with music lessons.

My mother's younger sister Pamela was a conservatoire pianist. She was brilliant and artistic and played the piano very well. My mother thought *she* could play quite well too – actually I don't think she could – but she insisted I have piano lessons because it was what young ladies did.

So this very charming woman by the name of Sheena Neame, a member of the brewing family, came to give me lessons. It took quite a while to get beyond the five finger exercises, because quite frankly I wasn't interested. I'd sit with the music in front of me and we'd play these little ditties. After that I was supposed to practice, obviously.

But I wouldn't. I used to go off and ride my pony instead, which was much more fun. There was no-one to force me to practice. I thought the whole thing was a frightful waste of time and didn't want to be an accomplished young lady in the first place!

Eventually poor Sheena said to my mother: "Nadine, this is a waste of my time and your money. She has no talent, she won't practice, it's all absolutely useless." So that was the end of my piano lessons. Hooray!

After Amama died Pa was head of the Russian Orthodox Church in exile. We always cerebrated the Church of England Easter *and* the Russian Orthodox Easter, which is the most important festival in the Orthodox Church.

For the Russian Orthodox Easter my father always gave me a little egg, either wooden or jewelled – sadly not a Fabergé one. In Russia it was a tradition for Pa and his relatives to give each other little Fabergé eggs to wear around their necks on a chain. You are supposed to have a little egg for every Easter of your life but I don't have enough. I suppose I've got about twenty, some of which Pa made and painted himself. Some are wooden and some are made from stones which he found. They are really sweet and I wear them in a bunch round my neck at Easter time, which is quite pretty.

We'd go to the Russian Church in Emperor's Gate in London, which is long gone now because the building belonged to the Church of

England. We would go in Mother's car, driven by a chauffeur. Mother had a friend who was a gynaecologist and he lived next door to the church, so we'd often go to him first and have a drink and sit on the roof garden. Then we'd go on to the service.

Papa, Mother and I stood with our lighted candles next to the rood screen at the top facing sideways on to the public. Above us was a huge gallery where people could go and stand for the service. In those days you never sat down, now they are a bit more lenient. People standing above me in the gallery had their candles lit and the hot wax would drop onto my face, or onto my clothes and it would sting, so I'd start making faces. My mother was brilliant at speaking without moving her lips. She would say to me out of the corner of her mouth – so that nobody could see she was talking – "Stop it! don't be so stupid! And you *smile*."

One was supposed to wear white or pale colours for the Easter service. I had to wear a pastel coat and the whole outfit was rather sweet. My mother wore a yellow coat. It was always certain colours. But when the service was over I usually had lots of little spots of wax all over my clothes from the candles above.

After church we'd go for a big feast at Count Kleinmichel's house in Philimore Gardens, where we had delicious things like *Kulich* – the traditional Easter bread topped with white icing and the symbol XB ('Christ is Risen') – and *Paskha,* the rich creamy dessert. Count Klein-michel was an old friend of the family and had been one of Amama's advisors.

Pa loved food but he also suffered from duodenal ulcers. Though they were treated and he was cured of them in the fifties, he didn't like sauces and rich food. He liked really well cooked plain food.

The kitchen at Provender was Papa's domain. He did all the every-day cooking for lunch and supper. If he wasn't there, Ivy, our cleaner who came in every day, took over. She was a very good cook.

As a child Pa had watched the French chefs in the Russian palaces, especially one particular chef who would travel with them from palace to palace. Pa did vegetables that were green and slightly *al dente* long before people caught on that this was a healthier way of cooking, and he'd beat fillet steaks to a thin ribbon and then cook them in pan very quickly, as the French do.

My mother did the OTT things when they were entertaining, a bit like in the TV cooking programme the 'Two Fat Ladies'. "A little bit of cream" meant a pint of cream went in; "Oh, just a little bit of butter" and a whole pound of butter was mixed in – that type of rich food. Mother made a wonderful Lobster Thermidor and similar dishes. It was really good.

Father would smoke in the kitchen. Way back he used to smoke Du Maurier cigarettes and he kept his melon seeds in their orange coloured boxes. Then he switched to Embassy, which were hideously strong. They used to give tokens with them and he got a lot of things with the tokens he collected – hideous china, hideous towels, a wheelbarrow – but he was terribly proud of it all. He smoked until I had my tonsils out in 1970, but I continued to smoke when he stopped.

I smoked from the age of eleven. I was allowed to smoke Benson & Hedges in front of my parents when I was fifteen, although I was only allowed to smoke in public from the age of seventeen. I stopped through my four pregnancies, and took it up each time after the first few weeks of breast feeding. My eldest son was appalled that I was so irresponsible. He doesn't smoke and never has.

Mother hated the smell of smoke. Occasionally, fag in mouth, Pa would be stirring a sauce he was making, and just occasionally my mother would come in at the wrong moment and see the ash falling into the pot. She was livid! But Mother, who didn't approve of smoking, thought it was very good for getting rid of germs.

In those days when you went to the cinema you were allowed to smoke, and Mother and I went to see various films. One that stands out in my mind was *Tom Jones* in 1963, which was totally unsuitable for a 13 year old. Albert Finney was so good-looking in the starring role. I think we saw it twice and she smoked throughout the film. She never smoked properly. She never inhaled, but just used to smoke and blow out because she thought the smoke around her would kill any germs.

There was a big table in the kitchen with a bench on one side and chairs on the other and we sat there to have lunch every day. Pa used to summon me to the table with a dog whistle. Mother summoned me by shrieking "*OLGA!*"

If it was just close family we ate in the kitchen, and if it was less close family members, or if Mother wanted 'to do the grand thing', we ate in the dining room. But I wasn't allowed to come to the table until about the age of twelve and then I had to learn how to behave.

Although Mother wouldn't allow me to read the newspapers until I was about ten or so, from the time when I was quite young I had to mix with my parents' friends. Papa always introduced me to people as 'Baby'. He never called me Olga, it was always Baby. Consequently, I was very confident and at ease with grown-ups. I was totally uninhibited and never shy.

In the 1950s everyone had cigarette boxes filled with cigarettes, so when people arrived they were given a gin and tonic and offered the box. As a child I would take it round. Generally speaking they were Senior Service untipped or Players cigarettes, and Vicky and I used to gather up handfuls of them, then go out on our donkeys into the woods and smoke them. The problem with untipped cigarettes was that the cigarette paper became attached to your bottom lip unless you were very careful, and when you peeled it off it really hurt, so you had a nasty sore on your lip. And it was obvious that you'd been up to something no good!

I had to have *very* good manners. I had to learn how to speak to people and how to make conversation. Mother was very keen on that.

She would say "A lady always knows how to lay a table." So from about the age of twelve I had to lay out all the silver cutlery and mats and make mitres out of the stiff linen napkins. The mats were beautiful, my father painted the Imperial Crown on them. They've all gone now, sadly.

Sometimes I'd be naughty at a lunch or dinner party, or she'd complain that I hadn't chatted enough with the guests. During the first course you speak to your partner on one side, then turn to the other side for the second course, and so on... So if I'd been what she described as *sulking*, she'd take me out to the kitchen, get hold of my arm and twist it in a burn.

When Mother was really old, she did it to my daughter. We were all sitting around the kitchen table and she thought my daughter was *me*, because she looks like I did when I was that age. My daughter was absolutely horrified.

At about the same time Mother also insisted that I had to know 'how to clean a lavatory'. She would repeat: "A house can be untidy, it can be dirty, but you go to the downstairs lavatory, or to a bathroom, and this is how they rate you. You've got to have clean lavatories, clean taps and a clean basin." It's something that has been quite useful in life, I have to say.

When my mother was on good form she was *very* funny and had everyone in stitches. She was *incredibly* generous, that's why she died penniless and in debt. But on a bad day, if you said the wrong word that upset her, her very pale-blue eyes went *icy*. You knew you were in trouble.

For instance, she'd much prefer me to swear than to say 'God'. To her that was blasphemy. So if I said something like, 'Oh, my God', her eyes would turn from pale blue to *ice*. Mother didn't like blasphemy. I remember when I was about five saying, "Damn!"

Mother was appalled. She said, "Strawberry jam. You say 'strawberry jam'. You never use that word."

When I was about seven I kept calling the gardener "You silly old bugger." I hadn't got a clue what it meant and I don't know where I got it from but for about two days I called everybody a silly old bugger.

By now my mother was really embarrassed, so she said, "Now listen darling, it's not something one says, but you know the bullocks in the field?" and I said, "Yes." "Well you know when one gets on top of the other." I nodded. "That's what it is."

Mother was a force to be reckoned with. Ever since she was young she didn't suffer fools gladly. If somebody displeased her she could cut them off for ever. I remember as a child being present at a lunch party in the Oak Room. Among the guests were quite a lot of French and Belgians, and I don't know how it came up, but the conversation turned to supporting the Queen. One of the Belgian men said that he wouldn't support the Queen – why should he? And Mother just rose up out of her chair and said: "Get out of my house and do not come back." That's what she would do if somebody upset her, she just ordered them out of the house.

In fact that particular guest did come back a few days later to grovel, so he was forgiven.

She had incredible style and flair. In those days you dressed up smartly to go to London, these days nobody bothers. But she always looked immaculate. She was quite able to wear old clothes when she was in the garden, but she always looked very glamorous when she went to a ball or a party.

My father was HIH – His Imperial Highness – but he never used his title. Generally he was quite happy with HH – His Highness – unless it was a big function. Pa didn't like London life but occasionally, to make my mother happy, he would dress up in medals and court kit and they'd go to one of the Guild functions in the City. He was always Prince Andrew and on his cheque book it said Andrew, Prince of Russia. But he preferred the quiet country life.

Mother gave lots of lunch parties in London at the Dorchester, which was a favourite of all of us. A lot of things in my life happened at the Dorchester, the Ritz or Claridges. She gave big tea parties at the Ritz and dinner parties at the Ritz Grill, but it's all changed now. I remember my fourteenth birthday being there. It wasn't exactly a birthday party because everyone there was about 110 years old apart from me!

When Mother received an invitation, or if somebody she didn't know wrote to her, she would always test the embossment on the paper by flicking it with her finger to see if it came off. She was testing the class of person – or their money. So I'm afraid, out of habit, when I get a business card or an invitation handed to me, I automatically can't help just having a little *feel*.

Occasionally when Mother felt like it we went to Le Touquet in France for the day. There was the most wonderful hotel that had incredible food. I can't remember what it was called but it was *the* hotel to go to in Le Touquet. It was easy to drive there, have lunch, wander round the town and then drive home again. Sometimes we would also go to the beach.

We did that trip a couple of times and then in 1962 Mother thought I needed some culture. By this time I was twelve years old and I wasn't at all interested in culture but Mother nevertheless decided that we would go to Le Touquet and then drive on to Paris. My friend Vicky, who was eleven, came with us, also the Sondes' gardener Mr Turner, who moonlighted as our chauffeur, his wife and one of his daughters. Mother had a Humber Super Snipe which Mr Turner drove, and Papa had an Austin 1100, so we took both cars and alternated who sat with whom.

The hotel in Le Touquet was beautiful. Vicky and I had a gorgeous room with the most glorious bathroom. We shared a room, and my parents were in a room each on either side, as Mother wanted a room to herself so she would sleep better.

Pa was a brilliant gambler. He had a formula and he always used to win at roulette, so one night they went to the casino.

Le Touquet had a wonderful beach, although when the tide was out there was a big sewage pipe between the beach and the sea pumping out sewage, so we couldn't get to the water. Vicky and I were stuck on the beach, the wind was awful and we sat under little tents for shelter. It wasn't much fun. Meanwhile, unbeknown to me, my parents went to the races.

That evening we called on the Jellicoes, friends of Mother's who had a house in Le Touquet for the summer, and then Mother decided we'd go to a famous fish restaurant. We had a tower of shellfish and I had an oyster for the first time. It was all very nice, I ate like a pig and so did Vicky.

We went back to our beautiful yellow satin room, I went to bed and there was no problem. During the night I woke up. "Vic, Vic, I'm going to be sick," I wailed.

"Well get up then Beak," she said. I was known as Beak, because there was an owl called Ollie Beak on television. "Get up and go and be sick." And I was sick. I puked all over the satin cover of her bed, her transistor radio and the carpet between the beds.

Then Vicky went along to my mother's room. Mother had taken a mild herbal sedative called Serebol. It was made by a cousin who was a chemist. She'd also drunk a lot of wine so she was sound asleep. I remember Vicky standing at the bottom of mother's bed yelling "Nadine! Olga's been sick. *NADINE!*"

The shouting became louder and louder, then eventually mother woke up and came to look. "You little beast! How could you do that? Why couldn't you have gone to the bathroom?"

So Mother scrubbed and scrubbed to try and get rid of the smell and clear it all up. The next day the hotel charged her for the satin covers and the satin flounce round the bottom of the bed. And Vicky's radio rusted very quickly and had to be thrown away.

The next day we drove to Paris and I was still feeling slightly unwell. We had a huge suite of rooms on the second floor of the Ritz, Mother's preferred hotel. She didn't like heights but she didn't want to be on the first floor because she thought people might be able to climb up to the balcony and get into our rooms.

But Vicky and I weren't interested in the beauty of Paris; we weren't interested in the Louvre or anything like that. We fell in love with the doorman, and also with the Swedish floor waiter (we ate in our rooms), so we were only interested in these very good looking boys. Mother was very annoyed.

We managed to see everything though. We travelled to Versailles and Fontainebleau and it was all very jolly but really we weren't terribly interested. The best thing was standing on the Alexander III Bridge, which has the huge beautiful Romanov eagles.

Mother was very keen on Napoleon. My grandmother and aunt both wrote books on Napoleon and his era but I've never been keen on him. So we went to all the places where Napoleon had lived and also to his tomb at Les Invalides. And then we came home in our two cars. It was an interesting exercise but, as my mother said later, "A total waste of money as all those girls wanted to do was to talk to the waiter and the doorman."

My parents, I presume, thought culture came naturally. I never went to the opera or the ballet. They never actually played proper music to me, and they never took me to the ballet until I was much older, by which time my tastes were already formed.

From 1955 to 1957 we had two maids, Betty and Pat, who lived in the servants' wing, which is the part that's now let out to tenants. One was an Elvis fan and the other was a Cliff Richard fan, so I used to be in the servants' hall listening to their music from the age of about six.

Then the sixties came along and the music was all the Beatles and the Stones. I was a member of the Beatles fan club and a member of the fan club of the television programme 'The man from U.N.C.L.E.' Oh boy, Napoleon Solo and Ilya Kuryakin!

So I didn't like classical music. I didn't understand it and nobody had bothered to educate me about it, because they assumed it would come to me naturally. My parents also assumed a love of art would be automatic, not realising that before the First World War it might have been natural, but it certainly wasn't in the sixties. Much to my mother's horror I was still only interested in ponies and horses.

My education might have been a little strange, but my parents *were* old fashioned. My father didn't really know much about 'conventional English' ways and how children were brought up in Britain. He used to mutter things like, "The British can't stand their children. They put them in the attics with the nannies in the freezing cold." And he said that way back, the servants in Britain were treated like *dirt* because they didn't have bathrooms or lavatories.

Whereas, unbelievably, the servants in the Russian palaces had bathrooms; the *serfs* might have been dying, but the servants who worked for the Tsar had *flushing* lavatories, decent bathrooms and central heating.

So Pa knew no better as far as education was concerned and my mother had such a terrible time at her boarding school, she really thought that what they were creating for me was nirvana. It never *occurred* to her that I would be ungrateful, that in sixty years' time I'd be writing about my upbringing in a negative way As far as she was concerned, it was the best she could give.

5

OUT INTO SOCIETY

T HE FIRST TIME I went to Scotland was in 1965 and I absolutely adored it. My mother and father had also spent a lot of time there. Father loved Scotland because it reminded him of Russia, particularly on the East Coast with its birch trees and pines.

We drove up to Harrogate in Mother's very pretty new Rolls, quite a large Silver Cloud 3, silver beige outside and with red seats inside, which she had recently bought. After spending the first night there we travelled along the Jedburgh Road, which was a switchback, to Perth. There were no motorways in Scotland then. The Forth Road Bridge wasn't built either, so we went over the Kincardine Bridge and finally reached the Isle of Skye Hotel in Perth, which was amazing. I remember smelling the Scottish air and I immediately fell in love with the place.

We spent a couple of days looking at the sights around there before continuing north to Dinnet. Mother wanted to stay at the hotel where Amama had stayed on her way to Balmoral, but of course the place was not at all like I was expecting. It had lino on the floors and there was only one bathroom.

Mother was frightfully proud as we drove past Balmoral. She kept pointing out the places where she and Pa used to go.

My mother always hired chauffeurs from Jack Barclay in Berkeley Square. The chauffeur was supposed to drive us up 'the Devil's Elbow', a notorious double hair-pin bend about eight miles from Balmoral. It was so steep that in those days people had to get out of the buses so that they could walk up it. It's been straightened out since then and a by-pass has been built, which is rather sad in a way.

I don't remember why, but my mother was driving as we went up the Devil's Elbow. Suddenly the chauffeur, who was sitting in the front alongside her, must have had a turn, because he became *really* strange and sank lower and lower under the dashboard.

Pa and I were sitting in the back and we thought it was hysterically funny. The man kept sinking further down, until finally he was sitting in the well where the feet go and he didn't appear again until we got to Dinnet. He was very odd.

It turned out he was having a nervous breakdown. Mother sent him back to London the next day. It was literally just before Dr Beeching, chairman of British Railways, did away with the little branch lines, so we put him on the train at Dinnet and he went to Aberdeen and then headed south.

The next day another chauffeur called Foster appeared. He was quite nice and he *wasn't* having a nervous breakdown, so he could cope. But it was quite amusing for my father and me to sit in the back of the car and watch my mother driving. Actually, she was quite a good driver. She couldn't park or anything like that, but she was all right on the roads.

When we went to Balmoral we were allowed to go all over the estate because Pa had received permission from the Queen via her Private Secretary, Sir Michael Adeane. At the time the Adeanes were living in Craigowan, which is the house where Amama lived during the war. They were very sweet and gave us a nice tea. I saw the woods where my parents got engaged, and we went down to Loch Muick to the little cottage which the Queen uses for barbeques now, and where my father used to spend a lot of time.

Years later, I used to visit Loch Muick from the other side of the water. Prince Charles wrote a book called *The Old Man of Lochnagar*. Lochnagar is actually a mountain next to Loch Muick.

Then we went up to Bettyhill, which is as far north as you can get. Way back, before she married my father, Mother had a fiancé who was into sports like hunting and cock-fighting. He was very good and very famous with his dogs, so mother used to have red setters and she would field trial with them up there.

When I was in Scotland I wasn't allowed to wear my jeans. I had to wear horrible tweed skirts because Mother said you wore tweeds in

Scotland. So there I was, aged fifteen but looking like eighty, wearing these horrible clothes.

I didn't realise that my mother had already arranged with Rosalind Harrison-Broadley, the Dowager of Deeside (her nickname was Rosalind Hammersmith Broadway) that I could go to *one* dance and also to the Aboyne Ball. This was during what was called the 'silly season'.

You had to be eighteen to go to the ball but I was allowed in provided that I left at midnight, like a proper little Cinderella. Mother had brought with her a very pretty pink taffeta ball gown which she had bought for me at Harrods. She had very good taste when it came to clothes, even when dressing her daughter.

After that we drove to the Station Hotel at Inverness, where we stayed while we visited Glencoe and Culloden. Glencoe was one of the spookiest places I've ever been to. The atmosphere was horrendous. I can see ghosts and I found the place seriously unpleasant. Culloden Moor was also really creepy, although it didn't have the very steep mountains with the valley below like Glencoe.

We then continued our journey to Loch Ness, where Mother and I went on a boat trip. It was very windy across the loch and her scarf blew off her head and disappeared into the water. "Oh well," she said, "Nessie can play with that."

In fact, some years earlier, my maternal grandmother Sylvia saw the Loch Ness monster from a window, through a mirror. Granny was there when she was young, researching and writing one of her books, and her hotel room overlooked the loch. She was sitting at her dressing table, which faced the window, pinning up her hair (I don't know where her maid was, she never travelled without her lady's maid) and suddenly she noticed something in the loch. It looked like a large upturned boat but then it disappeared.

When she came downstairs she said to the doorman, "That's very strange. In Finland we moor our boats securely, but there was a boat in the loch that just disappeared, it was upside down."

"Ah," he said, "you've seen the monster."

I do believe in the Loch Ness monster, because of the depth of the loch. It's three times deeper than the highest mountain around and the bottom of the loch is not just flat, it's got huge caves each side

1 Princess Olga, aged six months, on the lap of Grand Duchess Xenia, 1950.

2 Grand Duchess Xenia holding her oldest son, Prince Andrew.

3 Grand Duchess Xenia with her son Prince Andrew.

Below:
4 Grand Duchess Xenia with her two older children, Princess Irina and Prince Andrew, probably photographed by Grand Duke Alexander, whose uniform cap is lying on the table behind her.

5 Grand Duke Alexander Michaelovich and Grand Duchess Xenia Alexandrovna with their two older children, Princess Irina and Prince Andrew, photographed in Grand Duchess Xenia's boudoir in their Palace at 106 Moika Canal Embankment (Naberezhnaya Reki Moyki) St Petersburg.

6 Prince Andrew Alexandrovich (*far left*) with some of his siblings and children of neighbouring aristocrats, probably sons of Count Illarion Illarionovich Vorontsov-Dashkov (1877-1932) and Irina Vassilievna, neé Naryshkina.

7 Prince Andrew Alexandrovich in his naval cadet uniform, driving an .'automobile'.

8 Prince Rostislav Alexandrovich (1902-1978) with his tutor in Grand Duke Alexander's palace at 106 Moika Canal Embankment (Naberezhnaya Reki Moyki) St Petersburg.

9 Grand Duke Alexander
Michaelovich ca.1910.

10 *From left to right:* Prince Nikita, Princess Irina, Prince Andrew, Prince Dmitri,
Grand Duchess Xenia Alexandrovna, Prince Vassili, Prince Feodor,
Prince Rostislav, Grand Duke Alexander Michaelovich.

11 The courtyard of the estate Ai-Todor: to the left the 'Old House', built in the mid 1870s, and to the right the 'New House' (the 'Children's House'), built in 1912. Grand Duke Alexander Michaelovich inherited the estate from his mother in 1891.

12 Grand Duke Alexander Michaelovich's Crimean estate, Ai-Todor, with the Black Sea in the background and vineyards in the foreground.

13 All the children of Grand Duchess Xenia and Grand Duke Alexander: Princess Irina, Prince Andrew, Prince Feodor, Prince Nikita, Prince Dmitri, Prince Rostislav, Prince Vassili.

14 Grand Duchess Xenia with her husband, her siblings and her nieces at her husband's estate Ai-Todor in the Crimea.
From left to right: Grand Duchess Olga Alexandrovna, Emperor Nicholas II, Grand Duchess Xenia Alexandrovna, and Grand Duchesses Tatiana and Olga Nicolaievna.
In front: Grand Duke Alexander Michaelovich.

15 Prince Andrew in his military uniform. Prince Andrew began his military training as a naval cadet, but in 1915 he changed to the army and became a lieutenant in the Chevalier Guards.

Below:
16 The Dowager Empress Maria Feodorovna and one of her grandsons, probably Prince Rostislav, in the garden of the Elagin Palace in 1915. At the beginning of the First World War the Dowager Empress lived in the palace, and Xenia and her younger children stayed with her while Grand Duke Alexander was away because of the war.

17 The Dowager Empress Maria Feodorovna with her daughter Grand Duchess Xenia and her grandson Prince Nikita in the park of the Elagin Palace, Petrograd, 1915.

18 Princes Andrew (*to the right*) and Feodor in front of the Imperial estate of Livadia, photographed in 1918.

19 *HMS Marlborough*, which was sent by King George V to evacuate the Dowager Empress and her relatives from the Crimea in 1919.

20 Grand Duchess Xenia Alexandrovna on board *HMS Marlborough*. Behind her can be seen her granddaughter Princess Irina Felixovna Yusupova (daughter of Princess Irina Alexandrovna and Prince Felix Felixovich Yusupov).

21 The Dowager Empress Maria Feodorovna on board *HMS Marlborough*. In the background is the town of Yalta.

22 Grand Duchess Xenia with her children in exile, c.1948.
Standing in back row from left to right: Prince Feodor, Princess Irina, Prince Nikita, Grand Duchess Xenia, Prince Dmitri.
Seated in front row from left to right: Prince Rostislav, Prince Andrew and Prince Vassili, with one of his nephews, possibly Rostislav Rostislavovich.

23 Grand Duchess Xenia in her grace and favour residence Wilderness House, Hampton Court, c.1950.

24 Prince Felix Felixovich Yusupov and Princess Irina Alexandrovna in exile in France c.1950.

25 Grand Duke Kyrill Vladimirovich who, to the Dowager Empress's severe displeasure, proclaimed himself 'Emperor' in 1924.

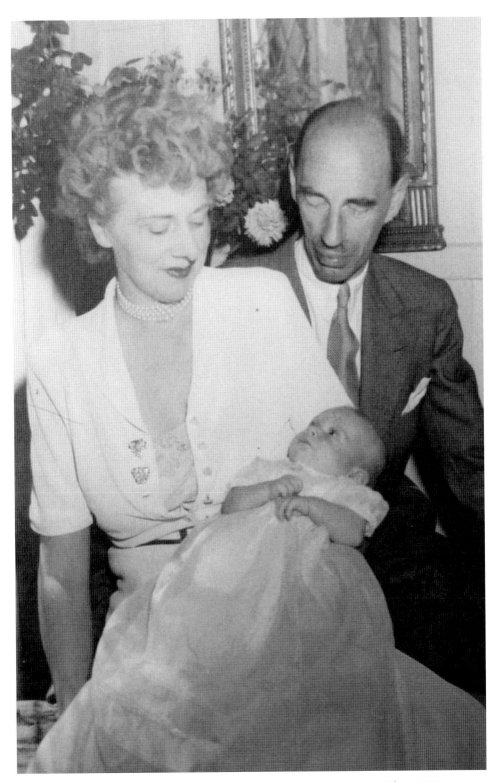

26 Prince and Princess Andrew with their daughter, Princess Olga, 1950.

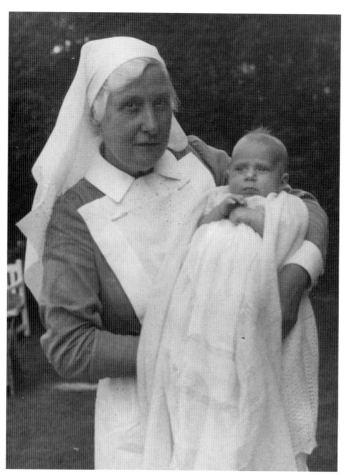

27 Sister Helen Rowe holding two-month-old Princess Olga.

Below:
28 Princess Olga with the daisy in her hand, aged six or seven months.

29 Princess Olga in the pram made by the Queen's coachbuilder, 1951.

Above:
30 Mother Martha, who looked after Grand Duchess Xenia, with Princess Olga and Prince Andrew, 1957.

31 Grand Duchess Xenia, her grandson Prince Alexander and Princess Margarita von Baden, holding Princess Olga.

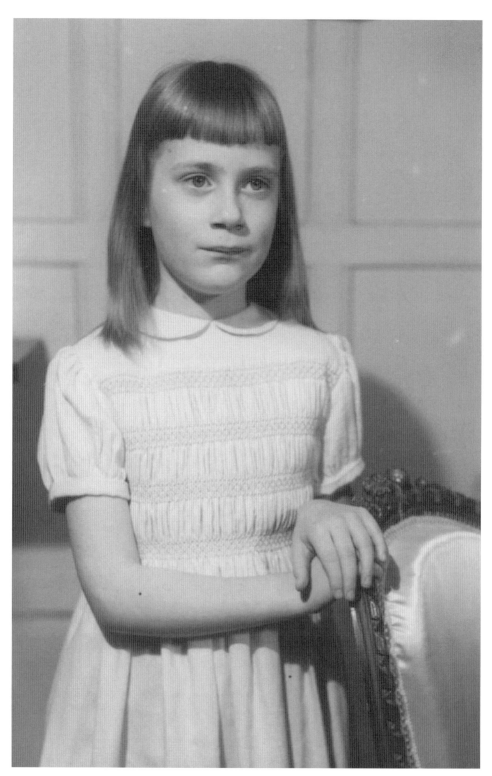

32 Princess Olga aged 7.

33 Princess Olga's 'darling Nanny Ray', 1959.

34 Princess Andrew on Chasseur, borrowed for the photoshoot.

35 Princess Olga riding out of
Provender on the donkey
Neddy, with her foal.

36 Princess
Olga on
Tina, the
pony on
which
she learnt
to ride.

37 Princess Olga and Thomas Mathew outside the Orthodox Church in London
after their wedding ceremony in 1975.

38 Princess Andrew with her mother Sylvia McDougall (*left*)
and Grand Duchess Xenia (*right*) at Craigowan.

39 Princess Olga's daughter Alexandra holding her brother Tom, who is holding Oscar.

40 Princess Olga's sons Nick (*right*) and Fran (*left*) in ATC uniform, aged 16 and 15

41 Princess Olga with Nick *(right)* and Fran *(left)*, with Alexandra on her knee,
under her maternal grandmother's portrait at Banchory.

underneath. And I believe that at some point something lived there that has obviously bred.

In some ways I was a very spoilt child and I became obsessed, while we were in Scotland, with wanting a Highland Pony. I had to have a Highland Pony. So I went on and on about this pony.

In Drumnadrochit near Inverness there was a famous family who bred these Highland ponies and also pony trekked them. They used to win prizes at the Highland Show. Mother made an appointment and we went there and found a very pretty silver dun coloured pony with a stripe down its back rather like a donkey. It was called Warrior. I liked it and rode it – it was very sweet. Mother arranged that in a couple of weeks' time they would drive it all the way down to Kent. And they did.

A few years later, in about 1970, I was sitting in the Officers' Mess in Bridge of Don, the Highland Brigade barracks, and a guy walked in and said, "Hello Olga. I don't expect you remember me, but my mother sold you a pony." He had joined the Gordon Highlanders and was now one of the Officers in the Mess.

But this pony proved to be rather a handful. It chucked one friend off on the clinker track on the farm. She landed on the clinker and, although she's in her eighties now, she still has the clinker under her forehead. He kicked another very good friend of my parents badly on the knee. The pony was wearing trekking shoes, so when he kicked out, the corner of the shoe did a lot of damage right through her breeches. She was visiting Harley Street for a very long time undergoing painful operations.

It must have been shortly after that time, in 1966, that *Harpers & Queen* made a list of all the foreign princesses who might be suitable in age for Prince Charles to marry. I was one of them.

Of course, they never spoke to *me*. Instead they asked my mother what I was interested in and what my hobbies were. Mother thought it was not good enough to put down 'riding'. "That sort of thing is unfeminine," she told me. So she said 'tennis' – but I couldn't hit a tennis ball to save my life – and 'sculling'. When I read this article, I asked: "What the hell's 'sculling', Mother?" and she replied, "Rowing, of course."

"But I've never *sat* in a rowing boat in my life! I haven't got a clue!"

"No, but it *sounds* good," she insisted.

In the event I only met Prince Charles once and that was at a cocktail party in Scotland when I was seventeen.

Mother was very keen on etiquette and she had a list of what she referred to as sins. These were things that you were *not* to do when you went to stay with people or even when you were in your own house. She was very conscious of the fact that some servants had a really bad time depending on who the people were they were looking after, while others had quite a good time. So the sins were:

- When you go to the loo you never leave a skid mark. Use the brush to make sure the lavatory is left spotless.
- If you're making love don't leave a stain on the sheets. Take a towel with you, but do not use one of the towels from the house.
- If you happen to get the curse when you're staying in somebody else's house, find the housekeeper and apologise profusely if the sheets are stained, because you can't do anything to stop that.
- If you've been sitting on the sofa in the drawing room and there are cushions behind you, always tidy them before you leave the room. You don't want the servants to come in next day and see an untidy room so they think you are slovenly. She was very conscious of that until she was really old, which is quite sweet really.

My governess Mrs Ebbutt remained with us until I was sixteen. Then in 1967 my mother decided to send me to finishing school.

Mother used to make me walk up and down with books on my head when I was little, so I could learn to walk with my head high and glide like a lady. In Pa's nursery days, to get him and his brothers to sit up straight, a walking stick was put behind their back and hooked under their elbows so that they couldn't slouch. He tried it on me a few times too.

In theory I could walk properly and get in and out of a car without my knickers showing in a mini skirt. It was quite easy, I didn't need all that.

But Mother thought a finishing school which taught cooking would be a good thing – why, I cannot imagine – and flower arranging. It was the kind of flower arranging where you plonked a big flower in the middle and then plonked one each side to build a triangle, and then arrange the flowers around it – hideous!

So I was sent to Winkfield, a very famous finishing school near Windsor, which had been set up by Rosemary Hume and Constance Spry. It's gone now but it was running for about seventy years. Spry did the flowers, Hume did the cooking. They also had another branch in central London.

Before I went there my mother looked round it at *least* three times. The only reason I was allowed to go was because Lady Kingsdown, as she is now called, who is in her eighties and whose late husband was Governor of the Bank of England, had also been there. She went along with my mother and said, "I was here [back whenever it was], it's the most *wonderful* place; she'll be perfectly safe. You *must* send her; it'll be such fun for her." So my mother was persuaded to allow me to go and if it hadn't been for Rose I might still have been sitting here with my governess.

So in March 1967 I went off to a lovely country house at Winkfield, where in theory girls were taught how to be young ladies and housewives.

In those days the parents had to sign a book to say whether their daughters were allowed to go out in the evenings with young men, or whether they weren't – and of course I wasn't. My mother signed the book forbidding me to go out because Sandhurst was very close to Winkfield and she didn't want me sullied in any way. There was a nanny at the door. I wasn't allowed out, and that was that.

In fact, it was basically the same at home as well. I wasn't allowed out with people. First it was because of the cars. She was afraid of her one and only child being involved in a car crash. And then it was the fact that I might do something more than a kiss.

Despite this, finishing school was quite fun because I made some friends. It was jolly and it was just so lovely to be away.

The drawback was that in the kitchen we weren't allowed to use any kind of machinery to whip cream or eggs. We had to do it all by hand – I was quite resentful about that. They taught you how to make things like Bavarois, a dessert similar to Panna cotta that you probably would never do at home.

The course did include some typing, but not enough for me to be able to get a job. Those were the days of manual typewriters and you had to really push down on the keys. I had very long nails and they went woosh into the typewriter workings. The teacher was so cross with me. "Olga, cut your nails," she kept saying.

"I can't do that," I replied. "I've got parties to go to."

My parents, or least my mother, thought I was going to make a good marriage to a man who had money and possibly a title, and who I would be happy with. In that respect she was a modern Mrs Bennet. So I wasn't really taught to do anything useful, because my parents didn't expect that I would have to work. I regret their short-sightedness enormously.

I was at Winkfield for nearly a year, then I got glandular fever and gave it to at least four other girls. I was sick for quite a while. I came back to Provender and was pretty feeble for at least four or five weeks.

That must have been in the summer term. This was the big term, because when you came back in the autumn term you had to do your exams. So when I went back they said, "You can take your exams." But I'd missed such a huge chunk by then. I suspect I've got dyslexia or dyspraxia, because although I can do things if I'm not told to do them, if I'm under pressure to do something I can't do it. My mind just goes completely blank. So I didn't take any exams and that finished the finishing school for me.

I went to Royal Ascot in 1967. We had some local friends who bred racehorses *and* also raced them, which is quite unusual. You usually only breed, or you own and race. Our friends bred *and* owned *and* they raced. These were the days of famous names like the jockey Lester Piggot and the trainer Vincent O'Brien.

Our friends' horse won on the day before Ladies' Day. It was fantastic, a huge thing. My parents were there that day, as our friends had sweetly invited them to Ascot three days running. On Ladies' Day I was invited to accompany them. It was my first visit to Ascot and I was quite excited.

On her lighter side Mother had a really good eye for colour and clothes. From when I was around fourteen to eighteen she'd buy me an outfit. She always shopped at Hardy Amies and Hartnell and the clothes always fitted and looked good, even though at the time I said, "I won't wear that ..." But they were really lovely, as were the hats, shoes and all the accessories.

So Mother bought my outfit for Ascot. She would look at garments and know they were the right size. I was stick insect thin then, more like Twiggy, so most things fitted me and looked OK. She also bought my patent shoes, which were Charles Jourdan and they were her only mistake. To start with they fitted, but of course they were new and it was a very hot day, so my feet swelled – they were absolute agony.

The night before Ascot I decided to tint my hair. The next day my mother came with the chauffeur to pick me up from Winkfield. I came down the front steps wearing my yellow hat, my yellow coat and my yellow shoes – it sounds hideous but it was actually very pretty – and she looked at me and said, "Bloody hell! What have you done to your hair?"

I said, "Um ... a bit of a boo-boo actually," because my nice naturally blonde hair had gone almost black. I thought it was funny. She didn't.

Bing Crosby was at Ascot that year. During the afternoon Mother went up to him and said, "Oh Mr Crosby, I'm one of your lifelong fans. Please sign my race card for me." I was standing in the background thinking, "For God's sake, how embarrassing!" He was very charming, I have to say. He didn't glare or snarl like some of the celebrities do but was really pleasant.

My preferred clothes were rather more casual than my Ascot outfit though. I remember going into Harvey Nichols one day wearing jeans and a sweatshirt. The sales people took absolutely no notice of me whatsoever.

The next day I went back all dressed up in a mink coat, high heels and make-up. Then I took out my cheque book. When the sales people saw 'Princess Olga Romanoff' they were all over me like a rash. I said to them, "You couldn't be bothered to talk to me yesterday, so I don't wish to talk to you today." It was just like that scene in the Julia Roberts film *Pretty Woman*.

When the Season began in March 1968 I was still at Winkfield. Mother took a large party of people to the first debutante ball at the German Embassy. When the cabaret came on, Papa turned his chair round so he had his back to the stage and was facing the corner. Mother kept saying, "Andrew! Andrew! Will you turn yourself around and look at the cabaret!"

"No," he said, "the cabaret in the corner is much more interesting!"

And there was the youngest debutante, only sixteen, virtually having it off in the corner with her hairdresser, whom she later married and then divorced.

The next ball was at Blenheim Palace. Again Mother had taken a large party, including my two male cousins and a boy called Theo Mathew, who was the eldest of eleven children. Theo was very good looking. He had enormous charm, greenish hazel eyes and a dimple. He was also great fun – but he had a bad reputation. Mother didn't leave me alone with him because he jumped on anyone vaguely attractive, so he was a definite no-no as far as suitable young men to take me out to dinner were concerned – definitely off Mother's list. But that night he introduced me to his brother Thomas Mathew, who was also at the ball and I thought, "Oh God, he's far too nice ..." I liked naughty boys.

After the ball I didn't see Tommy much during the next few years. I did see Theo, because he was my late cousin's best friend and he came to Kent quite a lot.

I was a deb for that year, which was fine, except that my mother wanted me to be chaperoned. I wasn't allowed to go and stay at house-parties — and this was the Swinging Sixties, for goodness sake! She thought I might do something wrong, or might be seduced.

Virginity was quite high on my mother's bargaining list for trying to get me a good husband. She really did think I would make a brilliant marriage, and if news had got out that I wasn't virginal it would be bad. So there I was, the virginal little girl dressed in white, having to behave modestly. When I protested, "But Princess Anne's allowed to do that," she said, "That's quite different."

Attitudes hadn't really changed at that time. These days people don't give a fig but in those days virginity *was* quite important. The pill was around but it had only just come out. I wouldn't have taken it at the age of seventeen or eighteen because I would have been terrified. Most of the debs in my year were definitely *far* from pure. But I was very pure because I was so frightened of my mother. That was an excellent contraceptive, so I remained a virgin until I was twenty.

Of course Granny brought my mother up and because Granny was old when she had her children, Mother still had the Edwardian way of thinking and her advice was archaic. In Edwardian days people didn't have divorces. If you wanted an affair you had it with somebody else's husband. They could never marry you because they wouldn't leave their wives and cause an open scandal. In those days this was perfectly normal. A few years later Mother said to me, "Darling, you're of an age now, go out … do what you want … but the sin is to get caught. Never get caught. If you get into trouble come back to me and I will sort it out."

Papa's outlook was Imperial. He didn't really mind who I married as long as I was happy. When they had rows Mother used to say, "This child at least will make a good marriage, unlike your other children."

When I started to go out with boys in the late 1960s, Mother had a thing about 'safety in numbers'. It was part of her pre-war ideas. Nice young men took you to the theatre, nice young men took you to dances, but you didn't go out with the same young man twice otherwise people would think there was more to it. At the balls you had dance cards and she would say, "You have a maximum of two dances with the same man and be careful who you have the last dance with."

They still have dance cards for the big balls in Scotland, but not down in London. The Scottish balls have had them for a long time but the cards are not as nice as they used to be. At one time they were a hard folded card and there was always a pencil with a tassel on it. The Caledonian used to have them and also the Highland Ball in London.

Occasionally I'd find a boyfriend that I liked and would bring him home, but they were always wrong in Mother's eyes. She constantly found fault with them, except for two of them. But because I was a bolshie teenager I dropped them as soon as Mother said they were lovely. I can see now why she wanted me to marry a man with money, because none of us knew she had run out of money and she didn't want me to suffer in the way she'd suffered for a number of years.

Queen Charlotte's Ball was the highlight of the debutante season. It owes its origins to King George III. In May 1780 he decided to give a ball for his wife's birthday so a number of pretty, well-born girls were invited and presented to Queen Charlotte. It later became part of the whirl of balls, cocktail parties and other events designed to launch young girls onto the marriage market.

The ball has been known for many years as 'The Harlots' Hop'. It was always *the* big event of the year. There were about 150 debs coming out in my year and during the evening it was traditional for a group of girls to pull the eight foot high birthday cake into the ballroom. The organisers asked me to be one of them but my father said no, because the girls who pulled the cake in had to curtsey and he didn't want me to do that.

Mother took a big party along as usual and one of them was a chap known as 'The Weasle', who was a friend of my two male cousins. During the evening girls kept coming to sit on his lap at the table. Mother was livid. "This is not the way to behave," she said. "I do not want all these tarts draping themselves over your body, thank you very much, at *my* table." So this was frowned upon. Incidentally, he's now a changed man. He got married late and became a house husband.

After my deb year the organisers gave up 'The Harlots' Hop', but the girls who were coming out only attended it once anyway. The other balls like the Caledonian and the Highland Ball still take place and you would go every year. They weren't just deb balls, although the debs went in their particular year. You didn't have to wear white either – although white looks quite nice with the tartan sash when doing the Highland reels.

I enjoyed being a deb. It was fun but I couldn't do it in the way that would have let me make the most of it. The problem was that people didn't want to invite me to house parties with my mother in tow. I was allowed to go to balls, provided the chauffeur drove me there. The 'chauffeur' was actually the local undertaker and often drove the car as slowly as if he was driving the hearse!

The poor man would drive from Provender to London, maybe three hours there and three hours back. I could snooze in the car, and I suppose he could sleep while I was at the ball. Then he had to drive me back, so that I was 'unsullied' and not groped. Also, Mother was obviously reading a lot of things about pot and other drugs. Many of my friends would go out and smoke pot – obviously she was petrified about the whole idea.

In July I had a huge coming-out ball at the Dorchester. In retrospect, I suppose I'm glad I didn't have a swimming pool as a present instead but it might have been of more use. People still talk about the ball though.

There were about 400 people, including Julian Fellowes who's now best known for being the screenwriter of the hugely successful TV series 'Downtown Abbey'. At that time he was still at Cambridge and to this day he says it was one of the best parties he has ever attended. Only about 150 of the guests were my friends, the rest were friends of my parents. It actually worked quite well because I believe in mixing the ages. My mother, not my father, thought it was a good opportunity to invite all the people she owed invitations and reciprocate that way, so she organised a *massive* fancy dress ball.

I chose the Regency period because I was very much into Georgette Heyer's books. Regency is fine when you're very thin, but it looks awful on a fatty. My mother unfortunately was plumpish. The men looked wonderful, because they had buckskin breeches and knee high boots, but the more buxom women *looked* even more buxom, because the Regency style dresses grab you under the boobs and then the skirt goes straight down. It was probably a mistake to choose Regency but I was thinking totally of myself.

My dress was white with puff sleeves, a green sash under the boobs and lovely little rosebuds all over it. Hardy Amies did it extremely well and it was very pretty, if you like that sort of virginal look! Eventually they took the rosebuds off so I could still wear the dress but without the embellishments.

I used to say to my mother, "Why do I always have to wear white to these balls? I hate it!"

"Oh, but it's the symbolism," she'd reply. The debutantes all wore white though, so it wasn't just me. "But I don't give a fig. I want to have colours." So occasionally, just as when I threw my toys out of the pram loud enough, I was allowed to have a coloured dress.

My father had his Regency suit made by Hardy Amies and then he went to Carnaby Street to get all the bits and pieces he needed to be a dandy. I remember him walking up Carnaby Street to buy a pair of shoes. My mother's dress was also made by Hardy Amies. In fact my mother's dress has been round the world with my wedding dress, also by Hardy Amies. The moths later got to my Regency dress and it fell apart.

The ball was a very grand affair. Tommy Mathew, his sister Elizabeth and brother Charles had hired a coach to arrive in, with two grey horses and a coachman. Theo came under his own steam. The coach was parked outside the front door of the Dorchester for a while. Elizabeth Taylor was staying in the hotel. Her young daughter asked for sugar lumps so that she could go out and feed the horses.

The whole thing was so glamorous. We had the big ballroom, which held hundreds of people, and the smaller ballroom which had tables, because Mother gave supper and then breakfast. The ball went on until 4 o'clock in the morning.

There was a room downstairs which they turned into a nightclub with a DJ playing the records. I wanted it nice and dark – those were the days! – but unfortunately my mother had already said to the people in charge, "Make sure the lights aren't too dim because I don't want any bad behaviour."

There was a dimmer switch, so we kept turning the lights down, then somebody else kept turning them up. Not bright, but so you could see who was doing what to whom. Mother didn't think too much darkness was fitting in case they groped each other. That was annoying but the ball was quite fun.

About three years ago I was sitting at a ball with my friend Georgie, Lady Colin Campbell. It was just about the time that various famous people were done for *squeezing*, now generally referred to as 'sexual harassment'. Georgie and I agreed: "Well, if we went to parties and we didn't get our breasts squeezed and our bums pinched we used to come away feeling totally affronted. It was perfectly *normal*." My son Fran thought this was the most appalling thing. He said, "Do you mean these people ...?" and I said, "Yes."

Generally it was one's parents' friends. All the old boys would come to Provender, and they would say "Hello darling" and give me a squeeze, but it never occurred to me that it was wrong. It was just perfectly accepted. Nowadays people would take a huge exception to it. Times have changed. Anyway, it doesn't concern me personally any more at my age!

I failed my driving test the first time because my instructor kept his hand on my knee. I was wearing a mini skirt and I didn't realise – I was so naive – that I was being abused. He put his hand on my knee and every time I changed gear his hand went on top of my hand. This rather put me off, so I failed.

Then we got an instructor from the British School of Motoring. He was totally professional and I passed in Herne Bay at my second attempt in early 1968. We went up to Scotland at the end of August and Mother bought me a white Mini Traveller with the number plate DSU 501G. It was nicknamed 'Don't Sound Upset'. Stiff upper lip at all times!

6

HIGHLAND FLING

I HAD FALLEN so much in love with Scotland that in 1967, when my maternal grandfather was dying, Mother sent me up there for the summer holidays to stay with Rosalind Harrison Broadley. One of her granddaughters was Davina Galica, the downhill skier in the 1960s, who then took up motor racing. I spent the whole summer up there, went to all the balls and absolutely adored it.

The following year I came out, so after my ball in 1968 Mother decided it would be fun to rent a house in Scotland for the summer so I could go to all the balls again. This was part of her plan for my 'brilliant marriage'.

Mother, being a frightful snob in that regard, thought I'd find a better class of husband in Scotland. Of course she wanted at least a Duke. She did have her eyes on Prince Charles, poor him. She wanted that type of man anyway. But as I was never introduced to any of the Dukes she wanted me to marry, I was hardly likely to be marrying any of them. Anyway, I said two fingers to all that.

So we went up to Scotland to look at a house to rent for six to eight weeks in the summer. First we went to see Kincardine House (now called Kincardine Castle) which belonged to the Bradfords. It was massive and quite old fashioned. The kitchen was in the basement, the dining room was quite a long way away and it had one of those dumb waiter pulleys that you put the food on in the kitchen and pull it up to the dining room. We didn't have any staff, there was just the three of us, and when Papa looked at the arrangements he said he couldn't *possibly* spend the summer in a house with a kitchen in the basement and the dining room miles away. No way.

Mother said we would look for another house to rent but there wasn't anything else suitable, so we decided to buy. My trustees said they would buy a house, it would be a good investment, so we began looking at various properties up and down that part of Deeside.

We were staying in the TorNaCoille Hotel in Banchory, a small village on the road to Balmoral about twenty-five miles from Aberdeen. Mother wanted to go and look at a little house in the village next to the primary school. She didn't want to turn up in her Rolls Bentley because she thought this would put the price up, so she borrowed a battered Mini from the hotel's owner.

We turned up at the house in the Mini and went round the property. When the owner had finished showing us around he opened the garage door – and there in the huge garage was a better and newer Rolls Bentley than Mother's! So she had to admit that she'd left hers in the car park at the hotel.

The house was called Gowanbrae. I think it cost £9,000 and we invested another £3,000 on renovations. It was a Victorian house built from granite, with two bay windows and three bedrooms. Mother knocked rooms together and did it up completely, so in the end it had three bathrooms as well. It was just stunning, straight out of *Harpers* or *House and Garden,* and was photographed everywhere.

There was a rather large walled garden with the most amazing orange roses called Orange Sensation, which my father loved. He created a kitchen garden at the bottom and it was great. We had lots of raspberries and other fruits and vegetables that year. Outside the front door was a weeping ash. When I lived up there years later with my children, I came back one day from shopping and heard a bleating noise – "*Mum, mum.*" I looked up and saw my five-year-old daughter high up in the middle of the tree. Her brothers had enticed her up and then taken away the ladder so she couldn't get down.

While the building work was going on we stayed in the TorNaCoille Hotel but Pa and I moved into Gowanbrae as soon as a couple of bedrooms and a bathroom were ready. Mother stayed on in the hotel, because she didn't want to be around all the dust and dirt.Towards the end of the renovation, when the builders were still there, Mother moved into the room that became our library. She lined the walls with plastic. Mother always travelled with this heavy plastic stuff which she put under the bottom blanket on a bed because she thought there was damp in other people's beds, and hotels had damp too. So she'd strip the bed and put on this crinkled stuff which made an awful noise when you turned over. It was vile! But she made the library nice and she stayed there with us until the house was finished.

We stayed in Scotland for the season of 1968. When I came back from a ball or a party, even if it was five o'clock in the morning, Mother would be waiting. Although she'd be in bed, she'd have one ear cocked listening for me. My room was opposite hers on the landing so she could see when I came in. She'd literally leap up and I'd have to give her a blow by blow account of the evening.

Pa couldn't stand the middle classes. He loved the working class and the aristocrats, but never had anything to do with the others. The class system now has totally changed though and the aristocrats have married people from all classes. But in Pa's day it was different. So when my mother was doing her thing with the great and the good in Scotland, Papa would say, "I don't want to go out tonight." And then he would invite the local butcher in, who was a darling, and they'd sit and have a few drams together. The middle classes, according to Pa, caused a lot of problems. Look at the Russian revolution.

The Oban Ball was in September. You had to have somebody in the neighbourhood to take the party along and preside over it, even though my mother was paying for the tickets. We had Jock, Viscount Massereene and Ferrard, who owned an estate on the Island of Mull and also, at that time, Chilham Castle, who obliged.

We arrived at the hotel in the afternoon but then it was announced that Princess Marina, Duchess of Kent, had died. My mother immediately said that she and Pa couldn't possibly go to the ball. I could go but, because the Court was in mourning, it was quite wrong for them to be seen dancing when Papa's cousin had died that day.

I went to the ball and they stayed in the hotel, which incidentally was quite vile. I had to share a room with my parents, and Mother snored for Britain! They had also brought along their six dogs. It was around five o'clock in the morning before I finally got to bed. Oban was where the McDougalls came from, so the next day we went to have lunch with the Clan Chief, who was female. First we went to see the old ruined Dunollie Castle, which was built in the twelfth century, and then we went down the road to the house where they lived, which looked out over the sea.

There was a big lunch laid on and I'd had maybe two hours' sleep because of Mother's snoring and my late night at the ball. So we sat at the dining room table, which was very wide, and there was a log fire behind me. The Clan Chief's husband was on my right, Mother was opposite – and I was so tired I went to sleep sitting upright, at the table, between courses.

My mother normally would have given me a really hard kick on the shins but she couldn't reach me because the table was so wide. So the first I knew was the lovely husband of the Clan Chief shaking my shoulders, saying, "It's all right dear, but wake up because the main course has come," and I said, "Oh my God, I'm so sorry." Mother was livid. She had that look on her face.

In 1968 the Guards' Depot at Ballater gave a small, fairly informal dance for Prince Charles and Princess Anne. They had quite a big dinner party beforehand for the young people, but although Charles and Anne were there I wasn't allowed to attend. Mother said that wasn't suitable.

"But *they're* there," I protested.

"That doesn't matter. You are going to have dinner with the Colonel and his friends." So I had to have dinner with the Colonel and all the righteous of Deeside, the youngest being fourteen years older than me. Then I went across the square to the dance.

Although I was never formally introduced to Princess Anne, she was aware of me because we were both attracted to the same handsome young subaltern. He would often escort one or other of us to various balls. At this particular dance we all came together in an Eightsome Reel. Anne and I were holding hands going round in a circle and, as we turned, she lifted the royal foot and walloped me on the shin. The pain was excruciating. I had the bruises for weeks.

Papa and I often travelled up and down to Scotland on our own. Sometimes we were lucky and the train went all the way to Aberdeen, but at certain times of the year you could only go to Perth.

At one time we had six dachshunds and they used to travel to Scotland with us and sleep on the bed in the dressing room. So we'd have all these dogs on the train. In theory dogs weren't allowed in the cabins but we got away with it because it was the prince travelling. It was such fun. Once we were bringing back so many dogs that we decided to fly, so we had to put them into crates. It was awful. They hated it, Papa hated it. He adored his dogs and was very upset.

At one time he had a miniature dachshund puppy called Hans, who would go in his pocket. Pa would go to the Ritz, or Claridges and the little dog would go everywhere. It sat in his suit pocket and its little face would just peer out, looking so sweet.

I lived in Scotland for three years, from 1968 until 1971. In the late 1960s, an unmarried girl who was even half attractive was a very rare thing on Deeside. The young people went away to school or university, so there weren't that many of them in the off season until they came home during the holidays. So I was a rare creature and very much sought after for dinners and parties.

Mother was very keen that people didn't think I was idle, so she got Jamie Burnett to employ me in his antique shop 'The Venture', in Dee Street, Banchory. I worked for four days a week from 9 to 5, supposedly selling antiques and bits and pieces like modern waste paper baskets and desk sets. Most of the time I would be huddled over the fan heater looking at the racing page with the guy from the shop next door, who would often pop in. Mother was terribly disapproving of this particular person for many reasons.

One day a woman came in and she obviously saw a muppet in charge – i.e. me – and she swapped the price labels on the stuff she was buying. Instead of giving me £60 as she should have done, she only gave me £15. I didn't realise this but in the evening when Jamie came to check up on how I'd done during the day he spotted it immediately. He was livid.

Jamie always came into the house for a dram on his way home

because he lived just up the road. For some reason our dachshunds used to bite him, particularly one of them. There were little fences about 12 to 18 inches high between various rooms and at the front door, so that the dachshunds couldn't get over. Jamie had a bit of a stammer, so he'd stand on the front door step and say to Mother: "Shut the f-f-f-fucking dogs up Nadine!" Only when they had been shut away would he come in.

On this particular evening he said he couldn't believe she could produce such a stupid daughter, and then went on to tell Mother what had happened. She was embarrassed and she loved Jamie, so she paid up. Poor Mother always paid up when she was embarrassed! I worked at 'The Venture' for about eight months but I wanted to stay in Scotland all the time. Mother said I couldn't possibly live in the house without a chaperone so Papa stayed with me.

Mother went south, leaving my father in charge, but she said I had to have an occupation; I couldn't just swan about enjoying myself because that didn't look right. She got hold of William Young and Co., a big antique dealer who had four floors in their shop in Belmont Street, Aberdeen, and arranged that I would work for them. But what I didn't know was that Mother was paying them to employ me. I didn't find this out until about two years after I'd left. I did think it was a bit strange that they didn't mind when I arrived late, or when all my friends from the Bridge of Don barracks came in and I was allowed off at lunch time longer than most people. I just thought they were very nice bosses.

I was supposedly selling antiques in their shop and I think I was useless. They had a very old fashioned camera, the kind where you put your head under a cloth and the camera was a huge box. So I'd take a photograph of an object and every week the advert went into *Country Life*. I quite enjoyed doing that.

Also they had a darkroom. One of the brothers taught me how to develop the pictures and I actually found that quite interesting. It's not a skill that's done me any good but it was fun at the time.

I can't remember how much money I got a week. I think it was about £5 for three days or some similar amount, but Mother paid it. When I found out I was furious.

This, of course, was the age of the mini skirt. Janet, the wife of my cousin Nikita, had bought one in Carnaby Street in the mid 1960s. She didn't like it so she gave it to me. Mother's reaction was fine. It wasn't very mini at all. But as time went on my skirts got shorter.

My criteria for a decent mini skirt was that when I stood up and bent my fingers the hem had to rest *inside* my fingers. It was a bit more decent than a pelmet. My father was very keen that I keep wearing my mini skirts. He liked good legs and he said if I wore mini skirts it would encourage my friends to come wearing them as well.

My mother, on the other hand, thought this was quite ghastly and that I looked like a tart. So when I lived with Papa in Scotland the skirts were very short. When I came down to Kent or was with my mother they dropped by about two inches.

I had a lot of friends in the Bridge of Don barracks, the Highland Brigade Depot. Women were not allowed to use the bathrooms in those days. I used to have dinner with various guys from the Bridge of Don so, as a courtesy, I was allowed by the President of the Mess to use the bathrooms after work. Though it was a strictly no-go area for women I was allowed to turn up and have a bath, because the President of the Mess Society loved me. I used to arrive after work, run the bath and put in a load of Floris oils I'd brought with me, but not everybody knew I was there. Occasionally one of the officers would come into the cubicle next door, smell the oils and say, "Bloody hell, what's that?" Then I would yell out, "It's OK, it's me!" It was a good laugh.

On one occasion one of the young officers, who thought the sun shone out of my backside, was parading his squadron on the parade ground. The great and the good were there, and we were all sitting on a dais with the Colonel of the Depot and other dignitaries. As the troops march past they normally have their eyes to the right so that they can look at the guests and the senior officer. Then, when they have passed, the commanding officer would tell them to look eyes straight ahead – but this young officer forgot to do that because he was staring at me. So all the troops got to the bottom of the parade ground and they were still eyes right! He was reprimanded but we did have a good giggle over it. In the end the Colonel and the Adjutant thought I had too much control over their subalterns and they decided to introduce some competition, so they brought another girl along. They thought we would hate each other but in actual fact we became best friends until she died.

Sue had been Miss Scotland for three years running until they changed the rules; she was seven years older than me, glamorous and beautiful. Her father was Professor R. V. Jones, a physicist who was one of Churchill's wartime boffins, responsible for bending the ray so that the doodlebug didn't come towards you. Sue Parenti was his eldest daughter. So the Depot's idea fell flat, because we became very naughty together. Sadly Sue died many years ago of pancreatic cancer.

I was out a lot and after two years Pa got fed up with it. I found the letters he wrote to my mother saying he was lonely, he missed her and Baby was always out. He couldn't stand it any longer.

By this time I was twenty, and until I was twenty-one I couldn't be alone in the house because Mother said only a tart lived on her own. So she decided I had to move in with friends on Deeside.

I spent nearly a year living with some friends who my mother knew I liked, and who she thought were very suitable chaperones. They lived along the river at the village of Kincardine O'Neil, commonly known as Kinca. It was lovely. I could stand and do the ironing on their porch and watch the jets come in below me as they flew up the river. I stayed there for the summer, and also went back afterwards. This was before mobile phones of course, so when I wanted to make a call I had to use the land line. During that summer quarter Robert, whose telephone bill was normally £30, was sent a bill for £74. He was absolutely livid! So my mother gave him a case of whisky as compensation.

After I was twenty-one I could do what I liked so I moved back into Gowanbrae. Tart or not, it was OK to live there alone by then. At certain times of the year Papa and Mama would be staying at Gowanbrae with me. If it wasn't a big dinner party when mother was 'doing the grand', Pa did the cooking. We lived a lot on fillet steak and grouse. I can remember whining and saying, "Oh, not fillet steak again!" or, "Oh, not grouse again!" We also had a lot of lobsters, which we bought down on the quay at Stonehaven. They were wonderful.

Pa did some amazing paintings when he was living in Scotland. Amama drew and also painted watercolours, so Father would also have had the education to paint and be artistically accomplished. His creativity extended to other things too. For instance, he designed the cover for granny's book *Let's Light the Candles*.

He had a desk in the window which overlooked Scolty Hill in Banchory and he did some really good paintings which he sold in the local art gallery in Aboyne. He was particularly good at landscapes and had exhibitions of his work. Some had been done way back before I was born, others were painted in Scotland and he sold them for quite a lot of money. You couldn't tell if they were Russia or Scotland, the scenery was so similar.

I have all his books of small paintings and also the caricatures. He did a *lot* of caricatures, including some of Mother and some famous people like Stalin and Hitler. He was very good at them. Pa would go to restaurants and if he saw a sight in the corner that he found ugly or revolting, he would draw it on the linen napkin. People thought it was so funny that the prince would do that, so it was all right and they didn't care. Pa also loved painting flowers, especially pansies. He said the face of every pansy was different.

Mother thought painting would come automatically to me. She didn't realize it was something that had to be taught. So in 1971 she thought it would be a good idea for me to broaden my mind and study some art, so she decided to send me to Florence.

My father wrote to Nicholas Romanoff, the head of the family, who was married to an Italian, to say I was coming to Italy so I could arrange to visit them. Nicholas's father Roman was Papa's cousin and head of the Romanov Family Association. He and Pa had been under house arrest together in the Crimea for a while and had written to each other all the time in the years since the revolution.

Before I went we had a big dinner party at Provender for my twenty-first birthday. It was the first time I'd ever heard my father give a speech and he said the sweetest things about his "darling daughter".

I went out to Italy and almost immediately met the man who I semi shacked up with. That meant I didn't visit Nicholas and I didn't study any art at all. The only thing I studied was this lover!

I was twenty-one. He was about forty-eight. His name was Alfio

Rapisardi and he was a very famous Italian artist whose speciality was horses and nudes. He was half Sicilian, half Tuscan and looked like Omar Sharif. Those were the days!

I lived in Via San Nicolo on the other side of the river Arno, which is so trendy now. He lived in Palazzo Verdi in Santa Croce. He had a wife, or at least an ex-wife – I always thought he was still married to her but apparently he wasn't. He said he'd never have done that to me.

I wasn't really into art and the culture scene, I just saw Alfio on a daily basis. I was allowed to drive his Dino Ferrari up and down the Autostrade del Sole to a place called Practica de Mare, which belonged to the Borghese family. He had a house in the town wall there. I had a really lovely time.

After a year in Florence I brought him back to stay at Provender. But Alfio refused to speak English. In those days I spoke Italian. Pa's Italian was a bit rusty, because it had been thirty-five years since he had last spoken it, but Mother didn't speak it at all. Yet Alfio and my mother got on like a house on fire. She liked the sound of her own voice and he liked to talk.

My mother had her own kitchen on the other side of the house, which is gone now. And Alfio and I would come into her kitchen and watch her cook, and they would talk to each other non-stop, neither speaking each other's language. Still they seemed to understand each other a bit. Papa of course spoke Italian to him.

Mother put Alfio in the best guestroom (which at the moment is a storeroom), where there's a ghost. During the first night he was disturbed a lot because the ghost kept opening and shutting the bedroom door. At first he thought it was me. But I was in the nursery, because that was my room until I was quite old.

You only have to stand on the floorboards between these rooms and they make the most appalling noise, so Mother would have known straight away. She had ears like a bat – it certainly wasn't me trying to get into his room. That's why I was put there. Mother wasn't taking any chances.

But nothing came of this relationship. Probably the age difference had something to do with it. I have a very short attention span with people too. Boredom sets in easily.

After I left Florence I didn't see Alfio for forty years. When I went back to see him, the paintings of his horses were still fine but his nudes … well, they were like opening up the middle pages of *Penthouse* magazine. They were really graphic.

Then I invited him to come and see me in England and paint me on my horse when I was dressed for hunting at the local Meet. He couldn't come the weekend of the hunt, so I sent him photographs of myself in my riding gear, properly dressed with my stock and everything, on my lovely little black mare.

He painted the most incredible wall hanging with three different versions of me on my horse. It's hanging on the China Landing at Provender. And although I'm wearing green and blue and all sorts of different coloured jackets, and in one of them the horse doesn't even have a bridle, at least I'm not sitting on horseback in the nude!

I went back to Florence twelve years ago and saw him again. I go back every now and then. He was a lovely man. He's well over ninety now.

A few years ago I was walking around the Winter Palace with Sveva, my cousin Nicholas's wife and she said, "Olga, let me ask you a question. Do you regret all those years ago that you didn't come and visit us in Tuscany when you were there?" and I replied, "Yes, I do actually." They all knew Alfio. I wish I'd done what my father wanted.

After I left Italy, I had a boyfriend in the Royal Navy and then I went to Germany. Pa had also written to his cousins the Hohenlohes in Darmstadt, and I wouldn't visit them either. I was very tiresome.

Then I stayed with my cousin Henry Sondes in Kitzbuhl and when I came back I decided to buy a BMW. I'd had a BMW 2002 for about three years and I went all over Greece in it, so I wanted another one.

I remembered that Theo Mathew had a contact at BMW and I'd be able to get a discount. So I rang up Theo – having not spoken to him for two or three years – and said, "Hello Baldy." He wasn't bald, he had a good head of hair, but because his name was Theobald his nickname was 'Baldy'.

He said he could get me a car and a silver BMW 2002 duly appeared. It took me about eight months to realise that it was actually about £1,000 more expensive buying it that way than if I'd just gone to the showroom. The second time I rang Theo, Tommy answered the phone and asked, "Where are you?"

"I'm in Queen's Gate, staying with friends," I replied.

"I'll come over and we'll go out for dinner." So we went out for dinner and the rest is history.

Being an only child, when I met the Mathew family I thought how lovely it would be to be a member of a family of eleven children with wonderful Christmases and New Years. I envisaged all this cosy kind of catalogue idea of Christmas. Of course, what I didn't realise was that they back-stab each other and they can hardly all be in a room together. I was a lonely only child at times, particularly after all my friends went off to boarding school, and I thought being in a big family would be just wonderful – but it didn't turn out that way.

7

PROVENDER

THERE HAS BEEN a house on this site since about the tenth century. My mother and grandmother liked to spin a yarn and say that the Black Prince lived here, because he's buried about twelve miles away in Canterbury Cathedral. But when the restoration work was going on we had lots of experts looking at the house and they said no, it definitely was not the Black Prince's shooting lodge.

In the thirteenth century Sir John de Provender bought the land and he and his son Elias built this house. It was a huge H-shaped building, much bigger than it is now, but it was always a medieval hall house, built on two floors above a central hall. The core of the house is thirteenth-century, and this includes the dining room which has a fireplace so wide you can climb up it. The workings of the spit are still up there. As a little girl I used to sit on the side by the roaring fire and watch the snowflakes coming down on my head.

Above the dining room are the Crown Post Room and the Crown Post bedroom, all dating from the thirteenth century.

When the restoration was being done and the roof had been taken off, the architects could tell how large the place had once been by the number of beams on the outside. In those days people showed their wealth on the outside of the house not on the inside, so the number of beams and how wide apart they were depended on how rich you were. The de Provenders were rich.

Then Lucas de Vienne bought the house. After him lots of other families followed, some of them Kentish, who all worked for the monarch on the throne at the time, until the Hugessens bought it from the family of Thomas Sare of Lenham.

The Hugessens were wealthy merchants. They and their descendants owned Provender for four hundred years and they were the owners for the longest. The Hugessen chapel is in the nearby Lynsted Church, the church to which my grandparents eloped and where my mother and her sisters were baptised.

We've got a weathervane in the form of a fox on the roof of the house because the Hugessens had the Provender Hunt. Many people had their own private hunt in those days. There were no roads; it was all big open countryside so it was ideal for hunting. When the Provender Hunt was disbanded about 150 years ago the hounds went to the Tickham, the local hunt, which was where my grandparents met.

The Hugessens also had their own cricket club, which has started again down the road and taken the name of the Provender Cricket Club. I'm the President.

But to go back to the history of the house, William Weston Hugessen left two daughters, who were co-heiresses. Dorothea Hugessen married Sir Joseph Banks, who took part in Captain Cook's voyage to the South Pacific on the *Endeavour* as his botanist. He lived here for a short while and planted the American hickory trees and the Spanish chestnut. He also planted a Banksia rose but one of my mother's useless gardeners killed that off.

Dorothea's sister Mary married Sir Edward Knatchbull, the 8th Baronet of Mersham in Kent. When Hugessen died in 1764 his daughters jointly inherited Provender. Sir Edward Knatchbull's family took the name Knatchbull-Hugessen and two or three generations of the family lived here.

Jane Austen's favourite niece Fanny Knight lived here too. Jane's brother Edward took the name Knight because his rich protector left him the money provided he took the name. The Knights are also a fairly local family.

Fanny married Edward Knatchbull-Hugessen, the 9th Baronet, who became the first Lord Brabourne. The local village is called Norton, which is the family name of the Brabournes. I've got a book of Jane Austen's letters to Fanny, which were addressed to her at Provender.

Edward and Fanny lived at Provender for a number of years, although she thought the house wasn't big enough for her servants. When Edward's father died they moved to Mersham. Fanny returned to Provender when she was widowed and apparently she created a wonderful garden, just like the one she had at Mersham. It's all gone now and nobody has any records of it, unfortunately.

When in 1890 the Brabournes were going through financial embarrassment, Lord Brabourne decided to rent out the house and some of the surrounding land together with the farm buildings. It was rented by my great-grandmother Constance Borgström (Lally).

As mentioned earlier, Provender was found for her by her brother-in-law, who lived locally. Lally had a coach and four and the horses were stabled in the barn. Then in 1912 the Brabournes' financial situation worsened further. They decided to sell off all the dower houses and land, and keep Mersham, so they put Provender on the market, together with the farm and all the farm houses.

My grandparents Sylvia and Herbert McDougall went to the auction to buy Provender on behalf of Lally. They were offered it all for a song but Granny was an awful snob and having been married to my grandfather, who was a soldiering farmer, she thought farming was all rather beneath her. So she said no thank you to the 400 acres and all the cottages and instead just bought Provender and 37 acres. That was very short sighted of her.

The farmhouse, which is fifteenth-century, was built for the benefit of the main house, so that they could grow their own crops and vegetables. All the windows face Provender. Even when I was a child, there were still bullocks in the bullock yards. And the back entrance for Provender House has been past the farm house for the last seven hundred years.

We've never found any secret passages inside the house. We do have smugglers' tunnels but they have never been opened during my lifetime. One tunnel has three entrances. One in this garden, one in the garden of the house opposite and one other – but we don't know which garden it's in.

When my mother was a little girl she went down the tunnel with the gardener holding a candle (when the candle went out you would know the oxygen had run out). They followed it quite a long way. It was beautifully arched and well built, with nice little red bricks, like the ice house we have in the grounds. Whether we'll ever be able to open it up I don't know. I rather think the military would have found anything of interest that was there, although it might have been blocked up before the war.

Sylvia planted a lovely rose garden. It was really beautiful and set out in a particular pattern. She actually did the digging herself, up to when she was about eighty, as well as dead-heading the roses and using her hoe. She was a proper gardener.

By the time Granny was in her late eighties, Mother literally had to go into the garden and drag her in, saying, "Mummy, you've got to come inside, or wear a hat, this is not good for you." Sylvia was a hard-working woman. She wasn't the type to just sit back and drink tea.

My grandmother died in 1962, and then the problems started. Neither the Finnish government nor the English government would forego the death duties. When Granny got to about eighty-nine she used to say to Mother, "I've got to go back to Finland."

"You're far too weak to do that," Mother would reply.

"Well, if I don't go, you're going to regret it," Granny always said.

And it was true. There *were* some papers she could have signed in Finland which would have simplified this business of the death duties. As it was, the matter dragged on for eleven years. Meanwhile, my mother ran up a lot of debts, thinking that everything would be all right in the end – but it *wasn't*. When the estate was finally settled, she didn't get very much money because of the long delay. And that was the beginning of the end.

My grandmother had what I call *quiet* sensible taste. She thought the house should be furnished to conform to the age of the building but when she died Mother wanted to change everything. She *loved* glitter and gold, and wanted to glitz up the house. She liked lots of bling. It was quite fashionable in the 1960s to have gold this and gold that.

She also wanted lots of gold and white because the Winter Palace, of course, is full of it. She didn't realise that Papa preferred to live in quiet comfort and that the Romanovs didn't live in grand style. They lived in the attics of their palaces which usually had fairly low ceilings. They looked like the lower middle class rooms that you'd find the maid living in, full of stuffed sofas with antimacassars on the back and palm plants everywhere. It was fashionable at the time but just awful compared to what they could have had. Unless it was a state visit or a function they didn't actually *use* the big rooms of the palace. I can understand that, but I think they could have had something slightly better and furnished them with more taste. Having said that, my bedroom at Provender is in the attic, and I enjoy it!

One of my grand friends said, "But Olga, why do you want to live in the attic? It's ridiculous. Why don't you take one of the better rooms on the first floor?"

And I replied: "Well, because it suits my personality."

So Mother thought she would make Father feel at home by making the house glitzy but Pa wasn't into the gold and the bling.

Mother inherited a little bit of money from my grandfather Herbert when he died in 1967, but not a great amount. In 1963 Herbert and his second wife Cicely had sold Cawston Manor and bought a beautiful large 4-storey house at 23 Wilton Crescent in London, which included 11 Wilton Row. We sometimes used to stay at Wilton Row, and it was lovely. They also had a big farm in Sussex.

Cicely was very intelligent, she was a blue stocking, and over quite a short period of time she made the Wilton Crescent house into flats and sold it all off. Then she sold Wilton Row.

I used to stay there in the 1970s. There were two or three bedroom flats, but Cicely kept one so that she could stay in London, and she kept the basement for the housekeeper to live in. When I stayed there I always wore my jeans as usual – but Cicely complained that it wasn't suitable for someone in Wilton Crescent to be seen leaving the front door in jeans and trainers!

When I pass by 23 Wilton Crescent now, and particularly when my daughter, who is a London estate agent, goes by, she says, "Oh my God, if only we still had it." It's worth many millions.

When grandfather died he left Mother *some* money in trust but Provender is a money pit. It cost a lot to run it then and it still does. Mother said in 1969 that it cost her between £25,000 and £30,000 a year to live at Provender, that included entertaining and probably her clothes.

That was one hell of a lot of money then! So eventually she was selling things and after Pa died she lived on virtually nothing.

However, *I* was set to inherit a lot of money from my grandfather from a big trust fund. But in 1970, when the house and Mother were in need of money, I was taken to a lawyer's office in Canterbury and asked to sign over the money to my mother. The lawyer was so horrified that he took me aside and said, "You do realise what you're doing, don't you?"

Money didn't mean anything to me then, so I just said, "Oh yes." I did it because I knew Mother wanted to be able to keep my father in the way *she* felt he should be kept. Also, as she was always telling me rather irritatingly, "You'll marry a rich man anyway."

In fact there were two trust funds that were broken, but in any case I'd have lost the money by now because I'm hopeless, still it would have been good to have it. Mother started to run into debt and had to sell the odd thing from the house.

She had already turned down one good offer years before. In 1964 a man turned up at the door in a big car. He was buying antiques for a collector and said to Mother, "I hear you've got a very nice Louis XV desk in the drawing room, a huge desk. I'll give you £34,000 cash for it."

Mother replied, "I'll have to think about it." She had connections and in those days you could do things you can't do now. She rang the bank and had him checked to see if he was good for the money, and he was.

She thought about it for a week and Pa and I were saying, "Take the money!" Of course, I didn't know about the debts, I was only fourteen. But £34,000 in 1964 was a lot of money.

Anyway, in the end she turned it down. Her father was still alive and she said, "I don't want it to get back to Daddy that I've been stupid with my money, so I'm going to say no." Years later she sold that desk at Sotheby's, where it only fetched 10 grand. It was so stupid.

But nobody knew about the debts. The relations in Finland didn't know that she had no money. Everybody *thought* Nadine was wealthy because she still *lived* as if she was; and, because she was Princess Andrew, everybody bent over backwards to accommodate her.

She entertained quite a lot, and she did it in the most royal way. She would hire people from the local hotel to serve the food and one of our gardeners acted as the butler.

In fact the gardener did everything. Before he came to us he used to work on the farm pruning the fruit trees. One day he asked the farmer for a pay rise and was only offered a pittance. He immediately came round here, knocked on the front door and said to Mother, "Can I work for you?" and Mother said, "Of course." So he became our gardener.

He'd been in the Royal Navy and he was wonderful. Over the years he became the chauffeur and would moonlight as the butler as well. And he was brilliant at making cocktails, because he'd worked for the Admiral on Bermuda as the naval equivalent of an army batman.

There are three acres of garden but most of it is wild now. Pa was practical as far as the garden was concerned. He had a sit-on mower which was like a tricycle. You sat on it and it had a roller behind and the blades were at the front. He loved that. He was great to spend time with in the garden. He loved lying in the sun. He was brown-eyed and black-haired so he never burnt, just went the colour of mahogany. He would get a tan while going up and down on the mower.

Pa also liked to make little bonfires here and there, deadheading the hydrangeas and then burning the leaves. My mother had a thing about fire – in fact an absolute horror of fire – so when she saw a trail of smoke in the air she'd rush out shouting, "No, you can't!" She was always saying no –"No, you can't do this, it's *my* garden, I won't allow you to do that, it's not safe."

Pa would reply, "But that's ridiculous, you've got to burn the stuff, you can't leave it." There were plenty of rows about the garden.

Like me, Pa loathed dressing up. He absolutely hated it. He liked to wear his old clothes the whole time, except when he had to be scrubbed up to go to London. His hat had oil all round it, the coat had holes in it and his trousers were dirty. Sometimes Mother would try to burn them and get rid of the hat and he'd find it and put it back on. He had lots of comfortable clothes with holes in. They did go to the cleaners occasionally though.

Often he would open the front door in these old clothes, or he'd be outside when unexpected guests arrived and they would look at this man and think he was the gardener. So when they got into to the house they would say to my mother, "Oh we were talking to the gardener outside," and Mother would reply, "Oh no, no, that's not the gardener – that's the prince." He was often mistaken for the gardener.

Also, he sort of grunted at them because his English accent wasn't that good. Pa didn't actually like speaking to people he didn't know or didn't really want to meet. He was quite happy to be mistaken for the gardener. He could go off and work in the kitchen garden.

He had a wonderful big Victorian greenhouse which had a little potting shed next to it with a boiler inside. The pipes went through into the greenhouse so he could keep it warm in the winter. Unfortunately the greenhouse was destroyed in the 1987 storm, but he grew wonderful things like Cantaloupe melons and courgettes. He absolutely adored spending time in there and it was a good way of getting out of my mother's way. He had very green fingers and was brilliant at growing things. He actually worked quite hard; he was not just an old man pottering around.

My mother didn't have green fingers. She was quite happy to pick fruit and dead-head the roses but, although she knew about gardening, she didn't want to do it. I have to say I'm the same. I love beautiful gardens, but sure as hell I don't want to cultivate them!

Mother entertained really beautifully. Her entertaining was *legendary*. But it was all done with smoke and mirrors. Pa was very astute and I think he probably realised how serious the situation was but there was not a lot he could do. They didn't have joint bank accounts, and he didn't tell me either. It wouldn't have done any good anyway.

Mother didn't talk about money, although way back she would hire and fire accountants who obviously told her what she should be doing to rectify the situation. I remember her in tears on the phone to a huge firm from London, and she told them in no uncertain terms where to go.

Every week Mother would receive a special envelope from Clydesdale Bank in Scotland with Scottish pound notes inside (this was between 1969 and 1980 when people in England didn't mind Scottish currency). She used this money for tipping people. She also used to send a taxi to Faversham to collect the shopping she'd ordered by telephone.

Father loved to take some of the cash into town to buy the meat and fish every day, but he didn't deal with any of the finances. He had been brought up in a different way, with somebody else paying for things, like the Queen. He was fleeced *twice* by two partners in connection with his handbag shop in the 1920s because of his lack of experience. He wasn't good with money.

My father was a great stamp collector. He knew a lot about stamps and always got the Stanley Gibbons catalogue whenever the new one came out. He built up his stamp collection by swapping with other collectors and at one point in the 1970s he sold all the stamps he had collected for quite a lot of money. He was very pleased because it was something *he'd* sold. Although Papa always put letters back into their envelopes, unfortunately most of the stamps from the envelopes have gone.

All the family collected stamps. My cousin Alexander, who lived with Amama in the 1950s, said that when a letter arrived at Wilderness House the question was never "Who's the letter from?" but "What's the stamp?"

Pa had a very good tongue-in-cheek sense of humour. But, as he had a foreign accent and looked quite foreign, people didn't always understand when he was being funny. He was completely deadpan. He mispronounced words and said things purposely to wind Mother up. He always said the English language was ridiculous, so would say things like, "Oh, Moomy (purposely mispronouncing 'Mummy'), there's a doooove (he pronounced it like 'drove' without the r) out there." Mother would get so cross with him.

When he was a child he and his cousins used to have farting and belching competitions just for fun, like children do. Pa could actually burp while he was speaking but people didn't realise what he was doing. So he'd be sitting at a grand lunch party or dinner party and he'd burp. And because his accent was so strong, people would ask, "What did you say, Prince Andrew?" Mother used to get so angry! She would give him a very dark look across the table.

Pa was severely deaf too. In Russia gun salutes were often fired and, being in the Chevalier Guards, he was frequently exposed to them. There were no such things as ear defenders in those days, so the noise damaged his hearing.

During the fifties the hearing aids were large – he had a huge box with pieces that went in his ears – but then over the years they became a lot smaller. He could hear my mother's voice – it was very strident – and of course if they were having a row and Mother's voice became too loud and shrill he just switched it off!

Pa loathed cocktail parties. The extra noise apparently doesn't work well for deaf people, even now with sophisticated modern hearing aids. So when he had to go to a cocktail party he just switched it off. But he could always hear my voice – and I suppose it is strident – but it's the pitch that he found easy to understand.

Pa enjoyed shooting. He liked to shoot the pigeons out of the bedroom window. That upset Mother because sometimes it would take her by surprise. The first she knew was *bang! bang!*

There is a local farmer, Arthur Finn, who used to own all the land round here, and his grandfather owned the farm. The grandfather didn't leave the farm to his children or grandchildren, they had to buy it back at auction. Arthur used to have a rough shoot, this must have been in the early to middle sixties. They still have it, although the birds aren't as good as they used to be.

One day my mother said to him, "Arthur, *do* invite Andrew. He *does* love to shoot." Well, Andrew did love to shoot but whether he actually *wanted* to do this didn't matter. So they had a good morning's shooting. Just down the way there's a rough patch where rare orchids grow. It's a very pretty place on a hill and, as it was the woodcock season, it was full of these birds on that particular day. So everyone moved off except for my father – I suspect because he was deaf and didn't hear the instruction. Arthur said they came back to look for him and found him just standing there gazing around him, because the whole situation reminded him of Russia. Not the shoots, because the shoots were magnificent in Russia, but the terrain, the scenery and all the woodcock.

We had a rather nice shotgun, a 16 bore, which is quite difficult to get hold of these days. It was a wedding present to my father from

Mother but sadly it was sold. I regretted seeing it go, because I loved shooting as well. Pa was very keen for me to learn to shoot. I was allowed to do so when we were in Scotland. I remember my mother saying, "Andrew, is this a good idea? It's not very feminine or ladylike, is it?"

He replied, "No, but it is a good idea. She needs to learn to shoot and fish." He thought women should be able to do these things.

On the other hand, he didn't think I should be a model in London. Mother said, "No, your father doesn't want you walking down a catwalk like a tart." That was a great shame as I was asked to model and my life might have been quite different.

My father much preferred to stay at home. One evening he and my mother were invited for a drink at the house of the local big-wigs because they wanted to introduce the prince to various people. But Pa didn't want to go out. He said he'd rather have dinner with the children – that was me and my fiancé – so Mother went off alone. We were drinking red wine, sitting at the table giggling, and Pa turned to us and said: "Well, they wanted a king to visit them but they got the lady in waiting!"

8

MY CHILDREN

I MARRIED Thomas Mathew in October 1975 in two churches within three hours. The first service was at the Russian Orthodox Church at Emperor's Gate in London where we had six crown bearers – they were all Tommy's brothers and his brother-in-law. There are no bridesmaids in the Orthodox ceremony, only crown bearers and a page who has to carry an Icon on a cushion in front of the bridal pair.

After the Orthodox service we went to my mother-in-law's flat for a short break, then on to the Roman Catholic Brompton Oratory for the second ceremony. There were only sixty people and the Oratory is very large, but there were beautiful flower decorations and the singing was lovely. The page boy was joined by two bridesmaids, both relatives of Tommy.

After church we had a wedding breakfast in the Dorchester for sixty people, mainly members of the Mathew family because there were so many of them. It was a beautiful day.

My first child Nicholas, who is now forty, was born at Queen Charlotte's Hospital on 6 December 1976 – St Nicholas's Day and Finnish Independence Day. He's called Nicholas, not because of Nicholas II, but after the Abbot of Downside, Nicholas Passmore, who said to me, "When you have your first son name him after me."

My waters burst while I was at Provender. Two weeks earlier a ceiling had come down in the Oak Room just above where the pianos were. So when my waters burst I remember coming to the top of the stairs shouting, "The waters have burst!" My mother and my husband thought I was talking about another ceiling coming down, so there was a lot of effing and blinding going on until they realised what had happened.

It was about six o'clock in the evening and we hadn't actually done a dummy run from Provender to Queen Charlotte's. In Imperial Russia, if a baby was late, the woman would be taken out in a carriage over a bumpy field to shake her up and bring on labour. But I didn't need shaking up, so my father said, "Be careful, don't go over any bumps or anything because that will bring the child on quicker."

So we set off but I had to stop for a pee at garages about three times, in labour, while we were driving up there. In those days garages were not as nice *en route* to London as they are now! But when we got to London fate was on our side, because the traffic lights were green all the way to Hammersmith.

I had an epidural as my mother had filled my head with terrors about coming through the ether. She did ring up Mr Lewis, who was the most wonderful gynaecologist, when I was pregnant – because this was what they did in Russia of course, but there you had the children at home – and she tried to book a room next to me in the private wing at Queen Charlotte's. Luckily, Mr Lewis said, "Oh no, I'm very sorry Princess Andrew but we don't do that sort of thing here. The rooms are for patients, not for the patients' entourage." Although nowadays I think that's not quite true in hospitals.

I went in and was so scared. I remember Mr Lewis saying, "Now dear, if you're polite to the nurses, they will be nice to you." I was wheeled into the delivery room, had the epidural and everything was easy-peasy. Nicholas popped out quite successfully at two o'clock.

A few hours after the birth I was jumping up and down and my parents were in the room by ten o'clock the next morning. And Papa said to Mother, "There's the son you never had."

Pa loved the children. Nick was born in December and it might have been May when I came down to Provender for the summer. Pa was hands on, he just loved being with the baby, but I think he found it a little off putting when, on occasions, I'd come downstairs as he was having his breakfast and decided to wash the child's bottom in the butler's sink (even though the children had their baths at night). They had proper nappies in those days; there were no disposable ones like now. Then I'd change Nick's nappy and put on a clean one, all on the kitchen table. In the end Pa asked me not do that while he was having his breakfast!

When Mother married my father, who was of course Russian Orthodox, she was the only bride not to convert to Russian Orthodoxy there and then. However she did convert when Nick was born because she thought that, as Pa was the head of the Russian Orthodox Church in exile, it would be nice to go to church with her eldest grandson.

Mother was quite religious in a strange way. When she died she had about twenty or so prayer books by her bed, about three Bibles and lots of books on religion. And although she was brought up in the Church of England, her mother was a convert to Catholicism *after* her divorce from Grandpa and the births of three children.

The Orthodox are not overly keen on the Roman Catholics, but the Catholics are very fond of the Orthodox. When I travel abroad I take communion in the Catholic Church, and what I like about the Catholic Church is that you know the format, wherever you are in the world. A pity it's not any longer in Latin, but that's fine.

I must have been nineteen or maybe twenty when I told our wonderful priest, Amama's *own* priest, Father George Cheremetiev, that I had had sex. He patted me and said, "No, it's all right, my dear." He was just *wonderful*. And then he said, "You know, you can get married *three times* without a problem in the Orthodox Church." And I thought: "*Yes!*"

My second child, who is nineteen months younger, is called Francis after my late father-in-law. They only have one name each.

Father was so pleased to spend time with Nick and then with Fran and he was very good with them. He was so pleased to have two more grandsons as he'd never seen his other grandchildren grow up because they were born in America. He did meet one of them, Alexei, who is my age. He had long hair and my mother made the taxi driver take him to a barber and have it cut off before he met his grandfather! That was cruel. In fact I was messaging Alexei recently. He and his wife have been married thirty years and I told them to come and visit me. And I added. "I promise I won't make you have your hair cut off!"

He replied, "That's all right, I like being humiliated."

My daughter Alexandra, who is two-and-three-quarter years younger than Fran, was born in April 1981. She was due on the day

Pa died but she was born three weeks early. Pa was desperate for a granddaughter. Sadly, he never got to meet her but Queen Charlotte's Hospital took a photograph when she was born. Pa died a week later and was buried with the photo of his granddaughter. He was thrilled with the children and he loved them all.

Mother absolutely adored Nick and he was very good with his grandmother. He used to come into her bed in the morning and sit looking at photograph albums with pictures of the Romanovs in Russia and she thought the sun shone out of his bum. Then I had Fran and he was a totally different kettle of fish. He didn't want to do things with his grandmother and as he grew up he was quite an edgy child and said exactly what he thought.

Mother always liked to be in control. I remember coming into the hall and finding her shaking him like a rat – he was nearly as tall as her and must have been about ten or eleven – like she used to shake me when she was angry with me. But Fran just laughed. He always laughed when he was chastised or smacked, to wind you up. So there he was laughing and I came into the hall and said, "No Mother, you can't do that, not to other people's children, not even your grand-children. You have to just talk to them but you can't touch them."

Then, when I was pregnant with my third child Alexandra, she said, "You can't *possibly* be having another, you'll lose control of your children."

I replied, "What do you mean, lose control of my children?"

She answered, "You know, one you can control, two is a bit difficult but three you'll never control!'

The first Christmas after Alex was born I had the flu and Mother locked us all in the nursery. Pa had died a few months earlier, Alex was eight months old and breastfeeding, and there was no heating in the house. So my mother put Nick, Fran, me and the baby into the nursery with a couple of heaters and locked the door from outside.

I was so ill. If I wanted anything I had to get out of bed and go to the mantelpiece to ring the old servant's bell that alerted the flags downstairs in the kitchen. Alex was fine because she was only on breast milk, I didn't want to eat but drank lots of fluid, and we all had pots in our rooms because mother didn't want us going out of the door and down the corridor to use the nursery bathroom.

Nick can still remember hearing the key turn and then occasionally his father would come up with plates of food for them. It was a nightmare because Mother didn't want the children touching anything in the house.

When I went back to Scotland, I decided I'd move into my own house at Banchory. It had been empty for years and had galloping dry rot. All in all I spent twenty-four years living there; the last time was eighteen years on the trot.

I took the boys out of their local school, St Peter's at Eaton Square, which was lovely, and moved up to Banchory, where they all went to the local primary school. They just had to go out of the back door of the house and there they were in the school. My daughter hadn't started school at that stage, but she was so miserable and jealous of her brothers that she was put into nursery school and she was happy there.

Mother's ideas of bringing up children and mine were *completely* different. When we'd come down from Scotland at weekends, or when I would stay with her at Provender for a few months, my children weren't allowed to touch *anything*. "*Don't* let them touch the antiques!" "Keep their fingers off that table!" They weren't allowed to range freely round the house without Mother in tow watching them and shouting "Don't! Don't!" So they were kept very much in the nursery wing. Although Mother and I loved each other dearly, it was hell.

A few years later we had a fourth child called Tom, who was conceived in Scotland and died in Scotland at the age of eighteen months. He was born with a very rare heart defect. Only one in 30,000 children has it. Instead of four chambers to the heart he only had three, so he was blue and we had to keep him alive until he was strong enough to be operated on.

While my husband and I were nursing him, I took my eye off the pulse as far as the other children were concerned, so they ran wild. Tom needed 24-hour care. He only slept for twenty minutes at a time and only drank one ounce at a time, so he would be in the crook of my arm with the bottle on the side during the night. Every twenty minutes he'd wake up and cry for a bit more, then go back to sleep again.

He was eight months old when he had the operation at the Royal Hospital for Sick Children in Edinburgh. The operation was called a Mustard, after Dr Mustard, a Canadian surgeon. They took some of the membrane from around his heart and built a baffle inside the heart to make four chambers, and everything seemed to be going swimmingly. There are children, presumably in their forties now, who are still running around after having had this operation. But tragically he was the only child in Britain to reject his own tissue. He died in intensive care on my daughter's eighth birthday and is buried in a beautiful churchyard in the little village of Banchory. On his grave it says, 'The wee manny', because that's what the doctor used to call him.

After primary school, the children all went to Banchory Academy when they were twelve. There was no money for school fees and in those days it had a very good reputation for education. It was the best state school in the league in Scotland, which was lucky.

Nick didn't know that his great-grandfather Sandro had founded the Russian Air Force but from the age of six he told me he wanted to fly. Along with his tractors he also had lots of Dinky planes, metal planes and plastic planes. He just adored them. When he was thirteen he joined the ATC, the Air Training Corps in Banchory, because his best friend had joined and persuaded him that it was a good idea. They weren't allowed to fly gliders until they were thirteen but he was in the ATC until he was seventeen. They were taught how to fly Chipmunks and he had a ball. Nick is left-handed so they had to get him a special rifle for a left-handed person. He was a very good shot and he loved the ATC.

Then he went to Aberdeen University to do geography. He joined the University Air Squadron and was doing his training at RAF Leuchars three days a week. The RAF didn't really care what you did providing it was something sensible and geography was quite useful because they did maps, amongst other things.

He left Aberdeen with a good degree and got into RAF Cranwell in Lincolnshire, which he absolutely loved. We went to his graduation ceremony. I came down from Scotland with Nick's girlfriend Jude and Fran; his father came up from London. Nick didn't say he was getting an award – I don't think he knew. We were just sitting in the auditorium when they announced that he had won the Sword of Merit and the cup, beating all the pilots and all the navigators. His marks were extremely high. It was a wonderful moment.

While he was training at RAF Leeming, they were flying Hawks, a 2-seater plane. One evening in October in 2000 or 2001, the telephone rang at home. It was Wing Commander Egerton: "I want to tell you that your son's had a bit of an accident."

"Oh God! what happened?"

"Well, they were training in the designated low flying area above Berwick on Tweed and they had a bird strike. The plane went into the ground and he had to eject."

My reaction was, "That's a bit more than a bit of an accident!"

He said that he was phoning "just to tell you that at the moment we think he's OK". This was about six o'clock in the evening and I was frantic. Eventually news came through that they had been picked up by a Sea King helicopter and taken to the Nottingham Spinal Unit, the RAF hospital they use for spinal injuries, and he was fine.

Nick told me that the worst part was being put on the board and strapped into the helicopter. Apparently he kept saying to the medics, "It's OK, I think I'm fine," but they replied, "No, this is procedure. We have to strap you in."

Later I heard what had happened. As they were flying low a seagull went through the cockpit and through the pilot's visor, knocking him out. Nick was sitting on dynamite. He counted milliseconds and then he pulled the eject handle, and up they went. The G force is 28, which is what causes the problems to the spine. People have had fractures or not been able to walk again from ejecting like this.

So up they went, and as they came down the pilot came round and saw his plane going into the ground. It was in all the papers. I remember Nick saying that it was five million pounds' worth of plane that went into the ground.

The end result was that he got patted on the back. The pilot's mother wept over him and said, "Thank you for saving my son's life," and everything was fine.

So thankfully Nick survived. He said being ejected was perhaps the thing that everybody dreads the most and the fact that he had done it and come through it was fortunate. His skills got better and better. He received an award from Martin Baker, the firm which make the ejection seats, a special tie and some things for his wall. He went to RAF Leuchars where there are three squadrons and spent twelve years there flying.

Nick got married in 2003 to a lovely Scottish girl. One evening, while he was at Aberdeen University, he came back from a ball in Edinburgh and said, "I've met the girl I'm going to marry."

I replied, "Yeah, yeah," because Nick changed his girlfriends like he changed his socks. I asked, "What's her name?"

"Jude," he replied.

For one moment, well until I met her parents, I had a vision of some latter-day hippy because I had in mind Jude as in the song 'Hey Jude', and I rather imagined the worst. They turned out to be *the* most respectable people. Her father is an accountant. I thought it was funny that I should expect 'Hey Jude' to come from hippy parents, but in fact her name is Judith, although she's always been known as Jude.

When my son met her, she was at Edinburgh University and they went out for quite a long time before they got married, in Scotland, the day after Nick's twenty-sixth birthday. The reception was at her parents' house at Kilmacolm, outside Glasgow. They bought a house at Auchtermuchty, known as Muchty.

I'm now a grandmother as they have three children. My eldest grandchild Thomas is just twelve, Lucy is ten, and the baby Isabella (known as Ella) is six. Not only are they beautiful, they're also really clever, nice and articulate.

Fran is a completely different character from his brother. He was full of mischief and into everything. He had the most amazing laugh that has grown with him and is truly infectious. You can hear it from a long way off. Once heard never forgotten!

When he was five years old, his father and I were sitting inside a friend's boat moored at St Katherine's Dock in London while the children were all playing on deck. Alex was about three and Nick was watching her, as was the man on the boat next door. Suddenly I heard what I thought was a can of cola being thrown into the water, then a man shouting, "Child overboard!"

We ran up the steps onto the deck as fast as we could and I saw the man on the next boat putting his arm into the very dark green water. As I ran up to him I was just in time to see some blond hair disappearing under the water. With horror I realised it was Fran's hair. Had we got there a few seconds later we would not have been able to see it, as he was sinking fast!

He was pulled out quickly and his father took him to Westminster hospital to see if he had swallowed any of the filthy water. Luckily Fran was fine, he didn't need his stomach pumped and he came home that evening. We learnt afterwards that the boys had been jumping from the bows to the duckboards and Fran, being only little, had misjudged the distance. The near drowning experience unfortunately put his reading back, because up to then he could read quite well.

A couple of weeks later my friend Clarry thought it would be fun to take a boat trip down the river to look at the *Cutty Sark* and have lunch in Greenwich. I remember Fran looking over the side of the boat at the swirling water while Clarry and I hung on to his anorak just in case!

'Clarry' was Clarissa Dickson Wright, perhaps most famous for her television cookery series 'Two Fat Ladies' with Jennifer Paterson. She has been a friend of my husband's since they were at dancing school together in the early fifties. I met her in the early eighties, just after I'd had my daughter. After her boyfriend died she had to leave his London flat, so she used to stay with us at Eaton Place, which was just around the corner. She would sleep on the long sofa in our large drawing room. She did like to drink and even kept gin in the tooth mug by the sofa. Once she was so desperate that she drank a bottle of my Chanel perfume. It *was* perfume too, not *Eau de Toilette*. I was very angry because it had just been given to me.

About a year after Fran nearly drowned he had an accident while Clarry was staying with us. Clarry was heating up the milk for Fran's hot chocolate on our stove. The handle of the milk saucepan was sticking out and while Clarry was hunting for her bottle of gin at the other end of the kitchen Fran got a chair and put it next to the stove. The saucepan handle caught in his sweater and the milk went all down his back.

We immediately took his clothes off, took him to the guest bathroom and put a cold shower on his back – and as I put the water on his back the skin came with it. The ambulance arrived but our apartment block had 99 stairs and there was no lift, so we had to get him down the stairs.

I went with him in the ambulance; it was the first time in my life I'd been in one. He was taken to Westminster Children's Hospital just round the corner and put into isolation because of the wound all down his back. When we visited him I remember Nick being jealous because Fran got lots of presents of games and things to play with. The burns have virtually faded now, but he was in hospital for quite a while.

But Fran has done so much in his life. He took a year out after leaving school at eighteen, and that year became the rest of his life. He went straight off to South Africa to stay with friends, work on a lion farm and an ostrich farm and go skydiving over Cape Town. Shortly after he came back, we went to Russia for Tsar Nicholas's funeral.

Then Fran trained to be a stuntman, which sadly ended in injury, leading him to become a photographer for many years. Both of these careers have taken him all over the world. He is now a personal trainer and lives in London.

Fran is the go-to man if something needs to be done, whether it is taking down trees, building something or just providing a shoulder to cry on. He's brilliant at putting things into proportion. When I think something is terrible he can always make me laugh and calm me down.

My daughter Alexandra is known as Poggy. When she was a baby her nickname was Piggy Poggy because she was breastfed *and* ate as well. Luckily the Piggy was dropped, so she's just Poggy now.

Poggy studied textile and fashion design with management for four years at Heriot-Watt University. She was based in Galashiels in the Scottish borders, where all the famous cashmere mills and the mining used to be, and she had an absolute ball. She loved doing it and at the end of the course she had a very good exhibition. She did really well.

Afterwards she went to work at Adams Children's Wear, and then Mothercare. Everything seemed to go well until there was a big full page spread of us in *Hello* magazine. After that they took a strong dislike to her at her workplace because they thought she was this posh bird, so she decided that the fashion world was rather bitchy and left.

Her father bought her a ticket to go to Australia and round the world, so she went off. But eight months later I had to summon her back, because a television company in England were doing a programme called 'Curious House Guests' and the producers wanted both of us in it. They liked the mother-daughter interaction and didn't want to do the programme without her. She's never forgiven me, because she was just about to get herself a visa and a permit to work in Australia.

She came back, became an estate agent and has gone onto bigger and better things. When she was working for one of the national estate agents she was voted the best sales person for that company. She's very good at her job and very good with people. She has more tact than me. She's now one of the best estate agents in London and has her own company. I'm proud of her.

Sometimes she reminds me of my mother and she makes me quite nervous because, although Mother died seventeen years ago when Poggy was nineteen, there are lots of things that Mother *couldn't* have said to her but they come out of her mouth. I am astounded. They are very similar.

Like me, Poggy can also sense the presence of ghosts. When she was working in Essex selling country houses she went to preview a new instruction. She picked up her London colleague from the station beforehand and they headed to the house. It was a beautiful day in that glorious summer where the temperature was in the high twenties. When they entered the house, Poggy felt the temperature drop dramatically in the drawing room. She was introduced to the owner, a woman, who within a few minutes asked her whether she believed in ghosts. Poggy nodded.

The woman then asked Poggy if she felt anything in that room. Then she said to her, "Let's play a game." She told Poggy to stand in front of the large inglenook fireplace facing the double oak doors, which the owner then closed. At that point Poggy felt as if a sledgehammer had been slammed against her back. There were goose bumps all over her. The owner told her, "Richard doesn't like those doors closed." 'Richard' was obviously a ghost.

They were then taken on a tour of the house. Suddenly the woman stopped and said to Poggy: "Your grandmother is very proud of you, she knows you hate being told what to do, but please listen to her advice."

Poggy thought, "Who is this nutcase?" but of course she continued to be pleasant as the woman was a valuable new client.

As they carried on looking round the property, Poggy and the owner continued to talk about which rooms felt as if they had a presence in them. Richard, the ghost from downstairs, had his own wing, which he haunted. It was a very surreal experience and by now Poggy's poor colleague from London was beginning to look quite spooked by their conversations.

When they were leaving, the woman asked Poggy if she could have a word in private, so off they trotted back to 'Richard's drawing room'. "From the moment you drove onto my drive, your grandmother has been bothering me," the woman said. "She *does* want you to listen to her, and she knows you are stubborn. She is so proud of you and is always watching over you."

"That's so nice," Poggy replied.

"Your grandmother isn't standing there by herself," the owner continued. "She is holding a little boy's hand. It's your brother. He too is very proud of you." At the mention of Tom, who died so young in such pain, Poggy burst into tears. She and the woman hugged each other while Poggy composed herself.

After apologising, the owner told Poggy that she couldn't control what she said. When spirits come to her she just speaks. She'd had this ability since she was a little girl. They then said goodbye and Poggy went outside to her car.

"Oh God, what have you done?" her colleague asked. "You'd better not have ruined this instruction for us."

"No," Poggy replied. "She was just telling me that my little brother and my grandmother are watching over me."

"What little brother?" he asked. "You haven't got one."

Poggy said it was a very weird experience. She loved the owner but, every time she went back to the house for a viewing, the woman would give more details about her life that no one else could possibly know.

The last time she went to the house, the owner opened the front door and said, "Your grandmother says take the job in London." That was one piece of advice that luckily my daughter did follow!

All my children joined the ATC and they all excelled in their various sports and their rifle shooting. Poggy swam for the school and played hockey for the ATC, so she'd go down South on the train on her own at the age of thirteen. Then later Benson & Hedges took over, so she was no longer as fast. Fran played badminton and Nick shot for the wing when he was in the ATC.

They are all exceedingly talented in their various ways, as are my grandchildren. Tom won a silver plate in a squash match a few weeks ago. Lucy came second overall running for the county. She's fast and has got very, very long legs, as has my daughter-in-law.

My children were brought up with animals but they don't have them now. Fran and Alex ride, but Nick thought one end bit and the other kicked, and it smelt in the middle. He did actually go out into the field in Scotland and he *could* catch the horse and bring it in. He wasn't really nervous but just wasn't interested in riding. Planes were more his thing.

During the four years he spent at Aberdeen University, he used to bring girlfriends back home. He'd say to them, "Mum's got a horse – do come out and you can ride it." So his poor little sister was sent on her pony to guide them and take them out.

Luckily when he met Jude, his future wife, she didn't ride and didn't like horses anyway, so that was never really necessary. My daughter-in-law is very conventional, a very good mother, a very good cook and a very long suffering wife.

9

PROVENDER
DETERIORATES

WHEN PA BECAME ILL he moved into the nursery at Provender, while Mother remained in her own room. One day, about six months before my father died, Mother rang me in tears, absolutely *floods* of tears.

I was in London and I said, "Oh my God, it's Pa," and she replied, "No, it's Sooty." Sooty was the black cat. I started to laugh, so she said I was very unfeeling and put the telephone down on me.

What had happened was that Mother was in bed with flu and somebody came up the drive and rang the doorbell. Ivy, the maid/cleaner, was there and she went to answer the door. Sometime later she came upstairs and said to my mother, "It was the wrong house, he wanted the farmhouse – oh, and by the way he ran over Sooty." Sooty was sitting behind the back wheel.

So Mother jumped out of her sickbed and called Papa. They went downstairs, scooped Sooty up off the gravel, put him in a box and called out the vet. He said, "I'm sorry, there's nothing we can do. He has to be put down." So he put him down.

Many years ago something similar had happened. My mother had a bull terrier called Cruncher. He was out in the field one day with Granny's Jersey cows, and Cruncher killed the calf of one of these Jerseys. Two years later Cruncher was out in the field and the Jersey tossed him up in the air, landed him on her horns and killed him.

Ivy, who was young then, walked into the hall and said to Granny and the assembled company, "Oh, by the way, Cruncher was killed by the cow." Forty or so years later she announced Sooty's demise in a similar way.

Pa died on 8 May 1981. It was an incredible shock. When my mother rang and told me I was really upset. In fact I haemorrhaged for about a month after Papa died, because I'd not long had a baby.

Because there was no Orthodox priest locally, Pa was given the last rites by a Polish priest, Father Edward Okan. He had been the server of Pope John Paul II when he'd been a parish priest in Krakow. Father Edward used to visit Pa weekly. They'd speak in Russian and chat about history. He was a lovely man, but of course he was a Roman Catholic. This caused some offence to the Russian Orthodox Church because Papa had been head of the Church in exile since his mother died in 1960. But in the circumstances, better a priest than no priest at all.

The Orthodox custom is that you lie in state in your house. The windows and all the mirrors are covered and there are four candles round the coffin. And the coffin is never left unattended.

It was a big funeral. We turned St Mary's, Norton into an Orthodox church. The Patriarch and lots of priests came down from London, and my brother Andrew came over from America.

Pa is buried in the churchyard. Also buried there are my great-grandmother Constance Borgström, my grandmother Sylvia, my grandfather Herbert McDougall and two great aunts. Next to Papa lies the older daughter of Field Marshal Mannerheim of Finland.

Peculiarly, Field Marshal Karl Mannerheim was one of the personal bodyguards of Nicholas II, as he was over a certain height. At Provender there's a photograph of him marching to the coronation next to the Tsar, and also a photograph of him in uniform when he became the Regent of Finland. He is the man who later freed Finland from the Russians. The Russians thought he had a big army, but in fact he only had a few men. So they rattled tin cans and made all sorts of noise to make the Russians think there were more of them.

He had two daughters, Anastasia (Stasi) and Sophie. Stasi was the elder and she was about a year younger than my father. Papa used to play with her in the palaces because Karl Mannerheim was also there with the Tsar. Years later Stasi became a nun and took a vow of silence. Later she had a nervous breakdown and left the convent.

My mother had also been friends with Field Marshal Mannerheim. In fact, I think she'd been a little in love with him once, as there are lots of letters between them. She was also friends with the daughter. When Stasi left the convent she bought a house in Hove, near Brighton, and my mother would take me there to visit her. Then, when she became really ill and old, she lived in a nursing home in Faversham and my mother would bring her to Provender on a regular basis.

For some years she'd been suffering from terrible shakes although she didn't have Parkinson's Disease. She couldn't hold a cup; she had to use a baby's beaker. When Nick was born she was so thrilled with Pa's grandson, and she adored me. My mother would say to me, "Let Stasi hold the baby, darling." And there was me, a rather Bolshie twenty-six-year-old, saying, "No." But she would insist, "Yes, let Stasi hold the baby, darling.' So in the end I gave her the baby. I remember him being dressed in a hideous turquoise babygrow. Because she shook so much, Nick adored it – it was like being in a cradle.

When she died the Finns didn't want her body back because she'd lived in Britain for fifty years. So she was buried next to my father, which is so strange as they were friends as children. The Finns do look after the grave though and we have a ceremony twice a year when they put flowers on it.

Pa had always said that when he died he wanted the Chevalier Guard vodka cups and the helmet to go back to the Chevalier Guard museum in Paris. Mother naturally wanted to carry out his wish but she had never been on a plane.

Sir James Cayzer, an old friend now sadly departed, decided it would be nice to take Mother and the stuff to Paris, stay at the Ritz for a few days to give her a break, and show her what flying was like. But Mother was very nervous. "I don't want to go on a plane, I don't want to go on a plane," she kept repeating. However, we went up to London and stayed in Claridges, which was owned by the Cayzer family, and the next morning she set off with Sir James. A few hours later I got a call from her in Paris.

"Well, apart from the walking to the plane, it wasn't bad and I spent the whole journey on the bridge."

I responded, "No, you silly woman, you spent the whole journey in the *cockpit!*" In the end the flight turned out to be quite successful, except she said she wouldn't want to do it again because you *did* have to walk miles.

Mother was always eccentric but as the money problems became worse over the years she became even more so. She went a little bit odd in her later years, but she was not exactly senile. I don't think she had Alzheimer's, but she became *much* trickier than she used to be, and she was pretty tricky when I was young.

Provender was always well heated until Pa died. He hated the cold because, although he was Russian, he was brought up with warmth in all the palaces. The winter after he died, Mother couldn't afford the oil for the heating and all the radiators cracked in the cold. She didn't have the money to repair the system so for two years she lived in this house without any heating – all she had was an electric fire in her bedroom. In fact she lived a very uncomfortable life in her latter years, just going from her bedroom and bathroom to her kitchen.

The water didn't work either. The gardener used to bring buckets of water upstairs and leave them outside her bedroom door so that she could flush the loo. It was bad. The house was so cold and there was no Aga to keep the kitchen warm.

But she was resilient and didn't suffer from colds very often. She'd had a tough upbringing, having been brought up in a house where she and her sisters had to break the ice in the pitcher by their beds in the mornings when they were little. Although there were lots of servants in the house the children's rooms were quite cold and fires were lit only occasionally. The adults had log fires.

People were quite sturdy in those days. I was brought up with central heating and my nursery was really warm, so I was lucky.

She missed my father *enormously*. No one really understands someone else's marriage. But they were devoted to each other in their own way and had a very strong bond. They also used to row a lot – well, my mother used to row with my father, but my father wasn't very good at arguing. It annoyed my mother. I'm like that too. A good fight can clear the air.

Mother lived alone after my father died. She spent a lot of time in church; she also spent a lot of time cleaning the graves in the churchyard. She was a very stubborn woman. She had no money, so bits and pieces would drop off the house. When the guttering fell off, she wouldn't put it back because she thought it would cost money.

At that time I was living in Scotland. About three times a year I would drive down with my dog to see her. I used to say to her: "Mum! That chimney… it's so rickety! The bricks are missing!" and "Bloody Hell, Mum, the tiles are missing!"

And she'd say, "Oh, don't be ridiculous, it's absolutely fine, this house has stood for seven hundred years without a problem and it'll stand for another seven hundred."

In January 2000 Mother became really ill, so I came back to live at Provender, bringing my chocolate coloured Labrador with me.

Mother was losing weight, she had a terrible pain in her upper back and after eating she was in agony – she also couldn't remember how much she'd eaten. She liked crème caramels from the local supermarket, so I'd get her six of these and she'd eat the lot.

She never talked about illness and refused to see a doctor. Way back, when I was about seventeen, she grabbed my hand one day and placed it on her Bible saying: "Swear you will never put me in hospital when I'm old!" Luckily she had a friend looking after her free of charge.

Her condition worsened very quickly and everything was failing. The doctor came out to see her and gave her morphine. He gave us enough morphine to set up a clinic but it was very difficult to get her to take it, so I had to put the liquid morphine in her whisky. It was a really horrible time.

When she was dying, I wanted to be present at her deathbed . Our friend Evelyn was holding her hand, so I said, "do you think I have time to walk the dog?"

"Yes," she replied, "go and walk the dog." It only took about ten minutes, but by the time I came back she had died.

Mother died on 6 June, the day after her 92nd birthday. She was buried in Norton churchyard next to Papa. My sons Nick and Fran were among the pallbearers.

I now had to decide whether to stay at Provender, which had become a semi ruin. It was so bad that the woodpeckers used to come into the house and I could hear them pecking their way *out*.

While I was deciding what to do, it seemed a good idea to have a break, so a few months after Mother died I went to Ireland to stay with a friend in Kildare who had seven sons.

On the last day they took me to a farm on my way back to the airport. As we were having lunch in the farm kitchen, a little black horse walked in, well its front bit walked in, and took a napkin off the table. I remarked: "Oh, how sweet" and went out to give it a hug. It was for sale but I didn't really think much about it at the time. Although I rode every day I didn't have my own horse at that time, I rode my friends' horses. So when I got home I told them about the little horse and said, "I think I'm going to buy it."

They were horrified. "But you haven't had it vetted, you haven't tried it, you've done nothing," they protested.

And I said, "Nah, it'll be all right."

So the horse came over here from Ireland on a lorry in July or August 2001 and she was the best thing I ever had. She's a pure bred Connemara but too big for the show ring. You don't back them until they're four and she was six, so she'd hunted for two years twice a week during the season.

She's got a grand name – Timahoe Sonata – because she's rather well bred. Timahoe is a stud in Kildare. We call her Sonny, because you can't stand in a field shouting, "Sonata!" You'd feel like a total idiot!

Now that I had a horse, my friend Fiona said, "we must go autumn hunting." I'd never done that before, having lived for nearly twenty years near Aberdeen, where there was no hunting. So once a week from August until 1 November we took the horses and a trailer and went autumn hunting.

The first time we went Sonny heard the hounds barking and the hunting horn sounding – and her little face lit up, she was so excited!

The Tickham was one of the oldest hunts in the country but it was disbanded five seasons ago, so we used to hunt with the East Kent. I hunted for two years before the ban, which was hunting as we'd always known it. I then hunted for three more years after the ban within the new rules. There were quite a lot of anti-hunting protestors around and we had to be quite careful, as they can trip up horses and other nasty tricks. After that the horse went off on loan. I couldn't afford to hunt any more so I haven't done it for seven years.

During the period I had Sonny, a friend's daughter, from the age of twelve, took her on and did eventing, dressage and pony clubbing. Sonny went as far as she could in all those things, then because she couldn't go any further, another child took her on. She school mistressed three different kids, as well as me (I used to have her just for hunting and hacking) – she was a real star. Everybody remembers her. She came back to me eventually and she's now out in my field.

10

RESTORATION

I DECIDED TO KEEP Provender not only because I loved it, but primarily because I wanted a challenge. Idle hands make light work and I knew that if I didn't have a project to keep me busy I would be getting into mischief.

The house wasn't worth much; it would only have sold for about £500,000 at that time. I had no income or savings, so I wouldn't have been able to live anywhere else. My only asset was this house, which I needed to turn into a business that would make me some money.

Provender is Grade II* Listed. The only reason it's not Grade I is because Mother thought the inspectors who came to assess its historic value were tradesmen and refused to let them over the front door step. Grade II* means it's a particularly important historic building of more than special interest.

However, the house was in a very bad state both inside and out and I had to find a way of restoring it. Then in October 2000 I was introduced to an architect called Ptolemy Dean. It's quite amusing how I met him.

Near Provender is the family home of my cousin Henry Sondes. The house is called Lees Court, and the back half and the stable block were designed by the architect Sir John Soane. Ptolemy happens to be *the* expert on Soane. He spent many years of his spare time researching in the Soane Museum and he's written many books about him. I didn't know any of this at the time.

Phyllis, my cousin by marriage, rang me up and said, "I want you to come to lunch at the big house because we've got a guest speaker coming who is an architect."

I replied, "No way am I coming to listen to some boring windbag and have to put a skirt on for the day!"

"Oh please, you're family, you've *got* to come," she pleaded.

My son Fran was at Provender at the time. He didn't have anything smart to wear to Lees Court, so he wore jeans and a leather jacket, I put on a skirt and we turned up for lunch. The guest of honour, Ptolemy, was late but when he walked in he was wearing jeans and a leather jacket and his hair was all over the place. It was love at first sight for all of us.

We all got on so well that I invited him to come and look at the house. He came round and absolutely adored it, so I asked him if he would consider taking me on as his client.

At that time he didn't have his own firm, so he went back to Richard Griffiths, the architectural practice in London he was working for, and asked if they would take on the job. And although they normally worked on churches and steeples and such things, they said yes.

Ptolemy took on the job in 2001. The first thing we did was contact Swale Borough Council in February that year. They gave me a grant to dig a French drain right round the house to dry out the foundations. By now the guttering had all fallen off, so the water came down and then back up through the foundations making the house damp, so the council allowed me to put up plastic guttering everywhere with down-pipes. That took quite a while.

We didn't actually start the restoration work until 2002, as we had first to raise funds. My previous trustees had said, "Don't touch English Heritage with a barge pole, they'll make life so difficult." But Ptolemy pointed out, "Olga, you've got no money, you want to keep the house, that's the only way forward," and introduced me to them.

The success of a project depends on the person who's in charge – and I must say I had a gem – so it all worked really well. English Heritage gave me nearly £400,000 which may seem a large sum, but the professional fees – those of Ptolemy, the structural engineer, the quantity surveyor and the archaeologists – accounted for a large part of it.

English Heritage call it 'Matching Finance' but in actual fact their contribution was only a fraction of the total. They paid for the restoration work in all the public rooms, the outside of the house and the roof.

We have spent just over £2½ million on this place, anyone else would have done more but it would have cost them £4 million. I managed to raise the money by selling things, including the field, so now I'm only left with 35½ acres.

Though the £400,000 doesn't come anywhere near the £2½ million I've spent, if I sell the house I have to repay the grant out of the proceeds. Provender is my only source of income, so I have to live very frugally, but it would be nice to be able to afford some champagne and buy nice clothes occasionally.

In making the grant, English Heritage recognised the importance of the architectural gems within the house, and we could start on the restoration work. Provender has about thirty rooms so we ended up dividing the work into four phases, but it takes an age to get things into gear when you're dealing with government bodies.

We had some hilarious times when we held the site meetings with the structural engineer and quantity surveyor plus the two architects, Ptolemy and Malcolm, and me in the kitchen. We usually adjourned to the pub afterwards for lunch!

Malcolm kindly helped my daughter Poggy clear out the attics. The attic which used to be two maid's rooms (and is now my bedroom) had lots of old carpets, rugs and other furnishings in it but everything had a particular smell – it was mouse pee and TCP. They had to keep going to the tip in Malcolm's old Ford to dispose of all this stuff. In the end, after numerous trips, he had to get rid of the car because it also smelt of mouse pee and TCP!

The first phase of the restoration was the seventeenth-century drawing room range. Then there was a gap because they had to send the work out for three different tenders, and they didn't necessarily choose the cheapest. The firms were interviewed by English Heritage, Ptolemy and Malcolm before the final one was chosen. I didn't care who they were, provided they were attractive to look at! I didn't always get my wish, although I was lucky most times.

Next they started work on the fifteenth-century wing where the tenant now lives, and then the third and fourth phases ran together. The third phase was the roof, although each time they did a section, the roof had to come off. Then they tackled the central core, the thirteenth-century part, which was the biggest job.

Finally, we came off the 'At Risk Register' in 2010 or 2011. Eventually we are going to do the brew house range. The brewery is where we're going to have a huge kitchen, while the nursery and my schoolroom are going to be turned into beautiful bedrooms with *en suite* bathrooms.

When they were working on the thirteenth-century part, there was no roof, just a scaffold with bubble wrap and a corrugated iron roof above it, so that the builders could work throughout the year. It took them about two and a half years to finish it. And that's when the ghosts became so tiresome.

Ptolemy believes in ghosts but Malcolm thought it was absolute nonsense – until one day when he was trying to shut a door in the thirteenth-century part and something was pulling hard on the other side. There was nobody else there.

On another occasion, when there was no roof, the builders were working in there and one of them shouted, "Oi!!" to what he thought was his mate, because a large chip of wood was thrown at his head. Again, there was no-one around.

The big mirror from the Crown Posts bedroom was put in the nursery corridor while they were renovating the room. It hadn't been cleaned for ages and was very dusty and was lying on its side. After a few weeks BEGONE was written in the dust on it, spelt as one word in the old English way.

The ghosts are in random places around the house. When my mother was alive our friend Clarry used to come down to Provender at weekends. There wasn't room for her to stay in the house because it was already collapsing, although we didn't really realise it, so she would stay in the farmhouse or with friends down the road. She always had to be given a bottle of gin though, as she was a great one for sitting up and drinking.

The first time she came here, my mother was whipping up a mayonnaise in the kitchen and taking care of the cooking, so Clarry was free to roam. Occasionally she'd come back to my mother and say,

"Oh, I've just seen the beautiful woman in the drawing room with an incredible dress and feathers in her hat." Then later she'd come back and say, "I've just seen her husband, the Cavalier, looking over the banisters on the back stairs."

My mother didn't want to admit there were ghosts here, because she lived alone and wasn't too keen on the idea. Though she didn't mind ghosts on one front, she didn't want them to be bothersome in any way. So she used to put all the stories down to Clarry's gin and alcohol fantasies, or the DTs – the *Delirium tremens* – the confusion alcoholics get as they withdraw from the drink.

Years later when Clarry was dried out and I used to stay with her at Inveresk, just outside Edinburgh, she'd say, "You know, it wasn't the gin talking," so she *had* seen the ghosts. She had also seen ghosts in other places.

I replied, "Yes, I know," because there were many generations of ghosts at Provender. The house is over seven hundred years old, so of course there'll be ghosts – people have been born here and have died here over the centuries.

Mother used to hear the furniture being pulled across the parquet floor in the drawing room. She'd rush downstairs (her bedroom was what is now the sitting room above) and open the door to see if anything was moving, or whom she could see, but she never saw any of them.

Also bells used to ring. We had a glass box up on the kitchen wall with flags, which connected to the rooms above. Often when we were sitting in the kitchen minding our own business, the bell would go for a room which we knew was locked up, and the flag would move.

I haven't seen any ghosts for a while. When my father was ill, I saw a grey lady without any feet floating down the gallery. A grey lady is a warning. White is good but when they're dressed in black it means death. But apparitions like that don't freak me out – our ghosts aren't malevolent.

Then there were the footprints. Granny's bedroom was off what is now the Crown Post rooms, which had a parquet floor. She had her own suite with a sitting-room, bedroom and bathroom. One morning in 1962, about three weeks before she died, we woke up to find wet footprints going from the gallery door to the top of the front stairs where there's another door. They went right across Granny's sitting room as well. The footprints were very narrow, as if dating from Elizabethan times, and they were quite wide apart. I was twelve and I remember standing in them.

Mother was furious that the lovely parquet was ruined, so Ivy, our wonderful cleaner/maid who had been with us since she was fourteen, got various products to try and remove them. Absolutely *nothing* would remove them. A few days before Granny died they disappeared.

There were two hollow oak pillars in the Crown Posts bedroom – they've gone now – with a French bed in the middle and a settle at the end – a kind of wooden bench with a high back. While Granny was unwell, I used to visit her. One day as I was coming out of her bedroom I glanced to the left, attracted by a rustling sound. I saw an old lady wearing a black dress, busily folding something in tissue paper on the settle. So I watched her for a while. As she moved her clothes rustled.

I came out onto the gallery and I said to my mother, "Ma, some old biddy in there dressed in black is folding something and her clothes are rustling."

"That's your great-grandmother," she replied.

My great-grandmother Constance went into deep mourning after her husband Emil died and never came out of black. So it was Lally, coming to see her daughter Sylvia as she was lying in bed waving, saying hello to people and looking very happy. She died shortly afterwards.

So first we had the footprints and then I saw my great grandmother coming to see her daughter.

The fifteenth-century wing was formerly the servants' wing. Between the wars it had six servants' rooms. Mother turned the old kitchen into a sitting room for Pa and his Russian treasures. It had red striped flock wallpaper, gold cornices and a skirting board and latterly became known as the Russian Wing. It was a big room and is now the sitting/dining room for the tenant.

The atmosphere in that part of the house is not welcoming. In fact we find it very unpleasant, especially in the bedroom. There are definitely ghosts there, and not necessarily nice ones.

Fran, Poggy and I can all see and feel the supernatural. Mother was the same, whereas my eldest son Nick wouldn't notice if a ghost came up and bit him on the bum. I think one of my granddaughters has the same ability. I believe children, until about the age of eight, can see and communicate with ghosts, talk to them and play with them, without realizing they're ghosts.

One Christmas, when my granddaughter Lucy was about eighteen or nineteen months old, she was outside with my son. Lucy could talk quite early and she was looking up at the window of the newly restored wing. Suddenly she started to scream, "Man with a white face!" Somebody was looking through the glass in the small bedroom which is quite a creepy place.

I let the fifteenth-century wing out now. For a while I had tenants in it who felt the ghost quite a lot. She was Polish and he was English. He said that often at around five o'clock in the morning he would see a woman standing by the window in their bedroom.

I asked him what century her clothes were, and if they were old. "No," he said. He thought she was probably wearing 1920s or 1930s clothes. We don't know who it was. "Did you touch her?" I asked.

"No fear!" he replied.

If he had been able to touch her, he'd have been out of there like a shot. There was something else there that used to turn the lights on and off. However nobody's been bothered by any ghosts since, except one can still feel this peculiar atmosphere. The present tenant has felt absolutely nothing.

The first tenant was a real East End roughie-toughie, a big man, and he had a friend also from the East End who dealt with fireplaces. Ella, his wife, told me the next day that this friend visited and he wanted to use the loo. In that wing there's only one loo and it's in the bathroom upstairs.

After visiting the loo, he came back down and said, "I don't know what you've got up there mate, but it's very cold and very peculiar. All the hairs on the back of my neck and on my arms went up. It's really odd." So they told him it must be the ghosts.

Ella told me that afterwards she walked upstairs wagging her finger and saying to the ghosts, "Naughty, naughty. You're not supposed to bother our guests."

The ghosts have been much better behaved since I threatened to sell them. After my mother died, I said to them, "If you upset me or my children, I'll sell the house – and you with it, to a wealthy foreigner."

On the whole they've been very good since then. But occasionally if my daughter comes down and she's unhappy about boyfriends, work or anything else, the extra energy this negativity produces triggers the ghosts.

The end of the gallery has a very uncomfortable atmosphere and a strange feeling also lingers in the Crown Posts bathroom, which you can also enter from the end of the gallery. When I, my daughter and Fran go down there we know there's something unpleasant because the hackles on our necks and arms go up. My daughter is particularly affected.

My maternal grandmother was a convert to Catholicism so I go and fetch her rosary beads, two of which had been blessed by the Pope, and put them on the door handles. I also put the statue of the Virgin Mary on the table. And within less than half an hour everything is peaceful again. It works every time!

I will never have my ghosts tampered with, nor did my mother, which was proved by the incident with the insurance assessor.

When Mother had her new bathroom built, a clothes airer was installed with an electric heater at the base and a pull-up wooden rack with a cover. One day in about 1957, while we were all downstairs having lunch, somebody knocked on the door and said, "There are flames coming out of the upstairs window." So we immediately dialled 999. Meanwhile, my father rushed upstairs and, remembering his army training, ducked under the flames with the Minimax fire extinguisher and put out the fire.

What had happened was that mother's stretchy nylon pants, which I suspect were much more combustible than the ones these days, had fallen down on to the heater at the bottom and caught alight. So after that we used to tease her. But she was very impressed with my father, who managed to duck under the flames and put out the fire.

As a result, the bathroom and the bedroom, with all her lovely satin covers and other such luxuries were ruined beyond repair, so she had to move into the best guest room. It took a good eight months before her suite was restored again.

Thereafter the Kent Fire Brigade used to come out to Provender on a regular basis because Mother was worried that they would take too long to get here if there was a fire. They treated it as an exercise to see how long it took them to get from the fire station to Provender, to get the hoses out and train them on the house.

After the fire, an insurance assessor came. On his second visit Mother left him alone for about ten minutes while she went to answer the telephone. When she came back to the drawing room the man said: "Oh, this room is so filled with people. I would *so* like to bring my wife here, my wife is a medium, you know. She would so love to chat to these people."

My mother just looked at him and said: "Get out of my house immediately! How *dare* you suggest my ghosts are tampered with, you rude little man!" And she shut him out of the house!

I feel like that too. The ghosts have every right to be here.

When I was twelve, we were coming back from the races and I saw a gnome. But the only person who understood was Clarry, because apparently there are people, especially the Irish, who do see these things. When I was telling my children this story, Nick said, "Please Mum, don't say that in front of my friends again because it's so embarrassing." But I did see a gnome. He *was* alive.

I also saw spacecraft in the garden long before helicopters were common. Papa always said there was life beyond this world and he very much believed in what are now called aliens, people who lived on other planets. I also think there's something out there. And I like the idea of conspiracy theories too.

There are a lot of *alleged* stories attached to this house. The fig tree in the garden is very old and there is a myth that goes with it. Allegedly, most of it died off before the First World War, but then it regained its beautiful foliage only for it to die off again before the Second World War.

At the moment, it's growing. It's enormous, I must get it cut back and pruned drastically, but I'm worried. I don't want to cause World War Three! Hopefully it's just a myth.

My life in this house now is hard work. There are no staff at Provender. I have a cleaner for three hours a week and a gardener who comes in once a fortnight. When Fran comes down from London, he's very helpful in the garden, having done some landscape gardening as one of his many jobs in London after he came back from South Africa.

I also take care of my horse, pony and dogs. I have two dogs now. One is a wire haired dachshund called Ronnie and the other is a Jack Russell called Jak. Ronnie doesn't actually belong to me. He belongs to friends, but because they moved and are always away working in London, Ronnie used to board with me. When they moved to Cambridge Ronnie became my dog. Luckily they pay the vet's fees, which are astronomical. Ronnie was bred to be a show dog, and inbreeding can cause health problems.

Provender is open to the public twenty-eight days a year. In addition, we have fifty people at a time for tea in the Oak Room, private groups, from April to October. During the summer I do the tours and people like to be shown around by the princess herself, so I have to try and be here. When I can't be here I have to grovel and send emails saying, "I'm terribly sorry I'm going to be away."

There's always an air of disappointment: "Oh, we *so* hoped to see you."

In the early days, when the house was first opened, the people who visited were mainly old ladies and people who generally just came to gawp at the place. But something was stolen right in front of my daughter's eyes!

Alex was at one end of the gallery by the doorway of the sitting room and I was at the other leading a group, so I couldn't see what they were doing behind me. But Alex saw a very respectable old lady from the W.I. put her hand out, then put something under her arm, and then as she walked down the gallery, into her handbag. Alex rushed down to the glass table and there was a mark where a box had been. It was *her* Russian papier maché box that had been taken. It wasn't valuable but it could have been Fabergé.

Instead of going to the group leader and saying, "I'm really sorry, but one of your members had just pinched something," I said nothing. But that put me off. So when English Heritage told me I had to have open days, I said I wouldn't let people range freely round the house anymore. And they agreed with me.

That was the only time anybody pocketed anything, but my daughter went around with a tray that evening and removed all the items she thought were of value and hid them. I was looking for them for two years.

She said, "No, I'm not telling you Mum, because you're useless and you'll get some more stuff pinched!"

Another time I was taking a group into the Oak Room and a little old lady turned to me and said, "Why is this room called the Oak Room?"

My normal reaction would be a Bridget Jones type retort about the blindingly obvious, but because they are paying for the tour I can't upset them. So I just smiled and said, "Well, if you look carefully, you will see that the whole room is lined in oak panelling."

Way back, before we opened to the public, Malcolm was showing some architectural people round the Russian Wing, which is now known as the West Wing. They had just come to have a look at the restoration work but the woodwork was still very rotten. A poor woman fell straight through the floorboards at the bottom of the stairs! It was quite a big drop but luckily she was really good about it and just laughed.

Once, when the nursery was included in the tour, a woman suddenly announced, "I don't feel very well," and fainted. Then she threw up in the first receptacle she found on the floor, which happened to be one of those small dustbins which my daughter had at university with her stuff still in it!

Occasionally people pass on interesting information. One tourist said that when he was working in a senior position in a famous, but now defunct, bank he and the other staff members had to sign a non-disclosure agreement about a certain account. The NDA had now run out, so he thought I should be told about it. Allegedly, Mrs Thatcher and Mikhail Gorbachev had formed their relationship on the proceeds of the Tsar's bank account which had gone unclaimed for seventy years.

Sometimes I enjoy doing the tours. It's quite hard work but I don't mind. The children have always said I like the sound of my own voice, so that's fair enough. The people who come to the house now are art historians, or just generally interested in architecture and history. Many of them are members of NADFAS – The National Association of

Decorative & Fine Arts Societies – so they're interesting people and I've learnt quite a bit from talking to them. All the architectural people know Ptolemy, and he is very highly regarded by them. They think he is God.

We also do weddings and events. We are planning a huge advertising campaign in the media. We have to make more than £4,000 a month minimum to be able to keep the house. So far I've made very little. The groups bring in a small amount of money, just enough to pay for some of the essential things. We're now aiming at bringing in enough funds to keep Provender alive for as long as possible.

One of my children is going to live at Provender and take on the various projects that I have initiated. Hopefully I will survive for many more years and see the house flourish once more.

11

LOST HERITAGE

IN 1919 *HMS Marlborough* departed from Yalta with my great-grandmother Dagmar, the Dowager Empress Marie Feodorovna, and other members of the family on board, including my grandmother Grand Duchess Xenia. They had very little time to pack, so they got out with only a fraction of their belongings, just some of their jewels and a few trinkets that they could sell.

My youngest uncle, Vassili, who was only about twelve at the time, brought his pet canary on board. Unfortunately, during the voyage one of his brothers let it out through the porthole and it flew off, never to be seen again.

At Provender I have two trunks which came with them on the *Marlborough*. One of them belonged to Amama Xenia – it's marked 'K' because the Russian alphabet doesn't have an 'X' – and the other one is Dagmar's and has the number '29' written on it. It shows how many trunks she had. They are beautiful inside but Dagmar's is the best one.

I've actually stood on the beach in Yalta. There's a memorial stone there now, which says: 'On April 11th 1919 the British battleship *HMS Marlborough* departed from Yalta taking into exile the surviving members of the Russian Imperial family, among them the Dowager Empress Marie Feodorovna.'

I remember thinking that they weren't exactly going on holiday. They *had* to leave. The *Marlborough* was only one of several warships, all crammed with people trying to get away from the Bolsheviks.

Dagmar only left because her sister Queen Alexandra begged her to go while there was still time. However, she didn't actually leave from the beach at Yalta where the stone is. She left from the cove at Koreiz, which is the Yusupovs' property just along the coast, because it was more private and secluded. She didn't want people to see her leaving, so the sailors ferried her out to the ship.

On board the *Marlborough* Xenia helped with the allocation of the cabins. All the crew, the Admiral, Captain and all the others had to sleep somewhere makeshift, because the cabins had to be given up for Dagmar and the other Romanovs. Dagmar was in a cabin on her own, but some of them had to sleep two, three or four to a cabin and Xenia's sons argued over who was going to sleep in which hammock. As well as the Romanovs there were other aristocratic friends, and also cousins such as Grand Duke Peter (grandfather of my cousins Nicholas and Dmitri) and his brother Nicholas ('Nicholasha'), the former Commander in Chief of the Russian army. They all had families, servants and tons of luggage.

Other ships arrived to help and people were standing on the pier at Yalta *pleading* to be taken on board. It was chaos.

As they sailed out to sea Amama borrowed the Captain's binoculars for one last look at the coastline. "What are those little black things all along the shore?" she asked.

"That is your silver, Madame," he replied.

The servants had been so afraid of being left behind that they had scrambled on board without loading the chests. There were fifty-four cases, and Amama and the others bitterly regretted their loss in later years.

They steamed first to Constantinople, where Peter, Nicholasha and their party transferred to another ship which would take them to Italy where their sister-in-law was Queen. When they left the *Marlborough* their places were taken by other refugees, so there was still little room to spare on board.

Britain still didn't want to give asylum to any Grand Dukes, and Dagmar probably didn't want to embarrass the British political and royal establishments. They steamed on to Malta which was British at that time. However, the crew were very good to my great-grandmother and her family. They organised an Easter Service on Good Friday and provided hand-painted eggs for Dagmar to give to the children on Easter Sunday, as is the Orthodox tradition.

They were all dropped off in Malta, much to my great-grand-mother's horror, because she hoped to be taken to England on the same ship. But the *Marlborough* was needed in the Black Sea and even a personal telegram from her to King George V was unable to alter this arrangement. So they had to remain in Malta until *HMS Lord Nelson* arrived to take them to England.

In Malta they stayed at the San Antonio Palace, which was the summer residence of the Governor. After being cooped up for so long during the revolution, Xenia's sons soon ran riot. The younger ones tickled the servants' legs at mealtimes and tugged at the rifles of the guards outside the palace, so they came crashing to the ground as their grandmother walked past. In strict defiance of the Governor's orders a young ADC was persuaded by a couple of the older ones to take them to the racecourse.

The older boys caused quite a bit of trouble. One evening a couple of them persuaded the chauffeur to park the open car outside on the road by the garden wall. They then crept out, climbed a tree, dropped into the car and drove into town. After an evening in Valletta, they made such a commotion when they returned that the ADC, wearing only his pyjamas, had to chase one of the boys to his room to make sure he went to bed. Another time my Uncle Feodor met up with Felix Yusupov and went on a tour of Valletta's night clubs with some of the *Marlborough's* crew.

San Antonio was famous for its lovely gardens and Dagmar was asked to plant a tree. While doing that she spotted the German Kaiser's name on a plaque nearby. "Why do you keep a tree planted by the Kaiser – horrid man!" she said, prodding it with her parasol.

"Well, it wasn't the tree's fault Ma'am," replied the young ADC cheekily.

Eventually the *Lord Nelson* arrived and took them to England.

Dagmar moved in with her sister Queen Alexandra at Marlborough House in London. But once they were in each other's company all day they fell out. They'd been like that since they were children.

By this time Alexandra was stone deaf. And while my great-grand-mother was *very* punctual, Alexandra was always *very* late. Dagmar thought because she was an Empress, she should take precedence over her sister, the Dowager Queen – that didn't go down well and the result was often a battle to be first through the door. In the end, my great-grandmother thought: "Enough of that! I'll go and live in my house in Copenhagen."

Dagmar went to Denmark and Amama stayed in England, so mother and daughter were separated, but Dagmar returned to London every year to see her sister. The problem of precedence did not disappear, however. After the wedding of the future King George VI and Queen Elizabeth, in 1923, Alexandra and Dagmar more or less *fought* each other to get to the front of the Buckingham Palace balcony.

Shortly afterwards Dagmar fell ill. So instead of going to Sandringham, Alexandra was forced to spend the whole summer at Marlborough House keeping her sister company until she was well enough to go home. It was very sad when they parted. They never met again as neither was able to travel any more.

Dagmar ended up living at a house called Hvidøre north of Copenhagen, which she and Alexandra had bought jointly in 1906. Before the war they spent a few weeks every year in this house to get away from court life in St Petersburg and London. It was *their* house. I have a beautiful portrait of Dagmar and Alexandra which hangs in the drawing room at Provender. It came from Hvidøre and people love it because of the vivid colours.

When Alexandra and Dagmar bought the house they put their favourite pieces of furniture in it. After Dagmar's death most of the contents were sold at auction but Amama and her sister Olga kept a few things for themselves, which is how we still have some of the Russian pieces Dagmar had kept there. These things went from Denmark to England, whereas we would never have been able to get them out if they had been in Russia.

Alexandra and Dagmar commissioned the now defunct furniture store Maples in London to make identical desks for them to go in the study which they shared at Hvidøre. I still have Alexandra's desk in the library at Provender – it used to be in Wilderness House. I don't know what happened to Dagmar's desk though.

When Dagmar left Russia her two trusted Cossacks, Yaschik and Poliakov, came with her. They left their families, followed her and used to sleep in front of her bedroom door. They died in Copenhagen and are buried there in a Russian cemetery. They were *so* loyal to her.

Dagmar's nephew, King Christian X of Denmark, who was rather careful with money, had to pay for the upkeep of Hvidøre and all the outgoings as his aunt had no money. Once, when she was spending the winter at Amalienborg because Hvidore was too cold, he tried to get her to have the lights on only in the room she was using. This annoyed Dagmar so much that she told her servants to run around and switch on *every* light in the house! I don't think Christian found that very amusing.

There must have been a lot of support behind the scenes for my great-grandmother because she lost her son and his family in the revolution – and many people felt this was tragic. So people came and paid court to her. Somewhere I've got the visitor's book with the names of all the people who called on her.

The jewel box and the jewels came to Denmark with her too. She never sold one piece of the jewellery, even though she needed money desperately. I still have this box, the one she hid under her skirts when the Bolsheviks came to search the house in the Crimea. It's beautifully made, a bit like a Fabergé piece, because the brass handle is set in so that it's flush with the box. It's made from purple leather and has a cover made from a type of canvas material. I don't have any of the jewellery though, sadly.

After Dagmar died in 1928, Amama and Olga sold the jewels – and nearly everything else – pretty quickly. And that's when old Queen Mary allegedly went to Hennells, the jewellers in Bond Street, the night before the sale and bought them at cut price.

Except, it turns out this story isn't true. The sales ledger shows that the jewellery was valued in 1929 *before* the Wall Street crash, and it was sold *after* the crash. But before the sale, it was *re*-valued. In fact Queen Mary paid more than the *re*-valuation price, so she didn't cheat the Romanovs. But nobody told *us* that.

For many years people *believed* that Queen Mary had bought the pieces at a cut price and that the present Queen, after she was crowned paid Amama the difference. That's what my Mother always told me. Now we know that the rumour was ill-founded. Sometimes I see members of the Royal family wearing Romanov jewels.

I've also got my father's trunk, which came out with him on *HMS Forsythe*. It's what one would call utility inside, as it's very bare and somebody ripped off the plaque on the top bearing his name a long time ago. I keep it in the passageway at home and it's very useful – I store clean old blankets and other things inside it.

We found Dagmar's diaries too. They were discovered by accident, in one of the cupboards in Mother's room and were sold to Slava Rostropovich, the famous cellist.

I also have in my possession a bottle of wine which came from Apapa's wonderful estate Ai-Todor, near Yalta in the Crimea. There were lots of different buildings on the estate, as well as thousands and thousands of acres of Sandro's own personal vineyard. The bottle of wine I still have is absolutely undrinkable though, because someone has pushed the cork through. I guess it would have been foul anyway because it's travelled so much and of course it's too old.

Apapa's vineyard had nothing to do with the Massandra winery. Although Massandra was one of the Tsar's palaces, the winery was founded by Prince Galitzine and was quite separate from the Ai-Todor vineyard.

I went to Ai-Todor in 2013 when I was doing a documentary for Ukrainian TV, while my son was living there. The Ukrainians first showed me Livadia, and then Massandra, which I liked slightly better because architecturally I found it more interesting. As we came round a corner I said, "Good God, this is an English rose garden!" and they replied, "Yes it is, because the Tsarina Alexandra wanted to make a garden the same as the one she knew from her childhood at her grand-mother Queen Victoria's home in England." They then showed me another palace. We visited three palaces in all, but all I wanted to see was Ai Todor.

I have so many photographs of the outside of Ai-Todor. There are also pictures of my father on his favourite horse which was shot by the Bolsheviks in front of him; in fact three of his horses were shot in front of him. The Ukrainians had never heard of Ai-Todor so it took them a long time to locate the place.

When we came to it there was a huge wooden security fence and an enormous gate with a little doorway set in it. The Ukrainian film crew kept banging and banging on the door without response. Then they rang someone who they thought might know how to gain access. Eventually someone phoned back to say that I would be allowed in with the interpreter, but not the film crew.

A nice young woman who spoke some English came and opened the door for us. We turned immediately left – and there were some graves in what is now a forest. Before the revolution it had been the chapel where my father had married his first wife Elsa all those years ago. The graves had been in the chapel floor.

Then we walked up the drive. At that time the place was a home for abused children aged between seven and eighteen. They had huge silos all the way up the drive – I trust they weren't nuclear – in which they had put windows and bunks.

We got to the 'big house', which wasn't actually that big and it was certainly no palace. An old lady came out to show us round. There were as many bunks as you could fit into these rooms both upstairs and downstairs. All the available space was taken up with them.

Then she told the interpreter in Russian, that before the revolution, seven children with their nannies would come and stay in this house – well, these children were my father and his siblings. Then the old lady pointed to 'the cookhouse' where the parents would stay, and we went across to see it.

In one quite small area there were three different houses. There was the chalet where Amama and Apapa lived, which was beautiful, like a Swiss chalet although slightly larger. It was so very wise of them to leave the children in the big house. Next door was the ancient cookhouse, which still had the frieze of hand painted drawings around the top where the cornice was.

Ai-Todor is now no longer a home for abused children. My cousin Misha Romanoff stayed there a couple of years ago and apparently it's been converted to some sort of spa.

My father loved Ai-Todor more than anywhere else in the world, and he loved the Crimea. As a child he used to run up and down the hill to the beach. It was all vineyards then. Now it's covered in hideous communist blocks rather than grape vines.

There's a path, now called the Sunny Path but originally The Tsar's Path, which runs all the way along the coast between Ai-Todor and the

Tsar's palace of Livadia. Amama and Apapa used it to visit the Tsar and his family.

Apapa owned thousands of acres of land. When my half-brother Andrew was in Ekaterinburg with the Americans digging up the bones of Tsar Nicholas and his family around 1989, he said to the Russians: "You do know that we own 90% of the vineyards in the Crimea?" It may not have been 90% but it was a huge percentage. And they replied: "Oh yes, we do know, but you've got to *prove* it". And I can't find *any* of the documents.

Apapa left the vineyards to my father and *somewhere* there are the deeds to the property, but I can't find them. I've searched everywhere. I've rung lots of lawyers but nobody could help me. The only thing I've found is a lawyer's letter to Papa, saying: 'Dear Andrew, here are six copies plus the original'. But there's no trace of the documents that came with the letter.

Back in the seventies my parents sold a trunkful of photographs at Sotheby's. My fear is that these deeds were amongst them, because they never thought then that they would ever need them again. So it's just possible they could have been sold with other papers and photographs.

Or maybe they're still sitting in a bank somewhere. The problem is that Mother changed her banks and her lawyers like she changed her underwear. I have had to go through every bank and lawyer that I can think of that Mother ever used. One bank said they had held some deeds but they were not there anymore. It's very frustrating, particularly now that the Crimea belongs to Russia again. Maybe someone will come forward one day to tell me they have the deeds – who knows? They are no use to anybody else. Even if we aren't given back the land, it would be good to get compensation at least.

One of the most poignant pieces I have is some china from the Ipatiev House. When the White Army reached Ekaterinburg in July 1918 they found no trace of the Tsar and his family. But in the house they found these plates, so they put some in their rucksacks and brought them back to Amama.

It isn't fantastic tableware but it's quite pretty. The Bolsheviks didn't want the Tsar and his family in captivity to eat off ornate china so it was about as plain as they could find amongst the Romanovs' crockery. It's white with a wide blue band around it, a narrow gold band and the

Imperial eagle. There aren't many pieces. They are now displayed on the China Landing, along with some of the white and gold china which was made by the Imperial Porcelain factory in St Petersburg for Dagmar and Alexander's wedding in 1866.

There was one icon which my father left me and which I thought had long gone. One day I found it wrapped in Dagmar's underwear. It wasn't ordinary underwear though. It was a special pair of crotchless pants made of lawn and gathered below the knee with a pink ribbon round them. And they had a special purpose.

Aunt Titti used to say that when they went to race meetings or similar events where they had to stand for a long time, they used to pee standing up, with people all around them. So they needed to wear these crotchless pants under their long skirts. It's a real skill and Titti was very good at it. But it's really difficult on hard ground as you get splash back. So the icon was wrapped in these special Imperial pants. There were two icons originally and they marked the escape of Alexander III and Dagmar from an accident. On 17 October 1888 the Imperial train was derailed and wrecked near Borki. A lot of people were killed and injured – they thought it was caused by a terrorists' bomb.

The Tsar had phenomenal strength, he used to tear up books and he could bend pokers for the children's amusement at Christmas. He wanted to get his family out of the train but the roof was crushed. So he held up the coach roof while his family and the nanny crawled out. This is what later killed him. It damaged his kidneys and he died of nephritis at Livadia in 1894.

After the train crash one icon was given to Dagmar and the other was given to Alexander. Dagmar's was a Fabergé starburst icon, an absolutely beautiful Triptych. It had rubies, sapphires, diamonds and a gold pattern. It was very famous. All the courtiers and friends who gave it to her had their names engraved on the back to mark her miraculous escape. I later sold it through an auction house in Sweden.

The icon was among the objects that I lent to an exhibition in Copenhagen in 2001. I went out there to see it and that was the first time I met the Queen of Denmark. Queen Margrethe is quite a close cousin, because we share the same great-great-grandparents, King

Christian IX and Queen Louise. She's a very nice and amusing woman, very natural and down to earth. She chain smokes and at that time I was also smoking.

We were in a beautiful room with amazing china on the walls and hanging in cabinets all around, and I went to put my cigarette ash into a bowl. "No, not in there! It's worth thousands!" she exclaimed, shoving a cheap ashtray in front of me. She was good fun. Her mother Queen Ingrid was my godmother.

I have also met The Queen a couple of times at parties. I think one of them was at a cocktail party at Abergeldie Castle. She remembered my grandmother and her visits to Wilderness House.

As a little girl I used to look at Amama's hand painted inventory of her personal jewellery. She had emeralds, rubies, sapphires and diamonds with stones the size of pigeon's eggs. They were incredibly large and really beautiful.

So when my mother said that my godfather King Haakon of Norway had given me a diamond brooch as a Christening present and Queen Ingrid of Denmark had given me an emerald and diamond bracelet, I was really excited. My childish mind conjured up all sorts of huge splendid jewels just like Amama's.

Then when I was about twelve years old the bank brought them out for me to see. I was very disappointed. They were tiny. The brooch was an H shape with a crown on the top in diamonds. It was very pretty, but small. It would have made a really nice tie pin. The bracelet was for a baby to wear, so it was very narrow. I eventually asked Wartski's to make it into a ring. I've still got it.

My other godparents also gave me presents that were more suitable for a child. I had a solid silver pusher, the sort a child would use with a spoon. It had a double AA on the front and it must have been given to me by Uncle Rostislav. It used to be in the night nursery. I remember using it in my highchair with one of those bunnykins bowls. It was a rather useful present.

A lot of the Romanov jewels and *objets d'art* were sold by the Soviet government. In the 1920s Emanuel Snowman of Wartski's in London went to Russia and bought up a lot of the Fabergé treasures. One of the things that he bought was the Fabergé egg with the coronation coach inside it.

One day Aunt Titti was at Wartski's with my father and they told her about the egg. "Oh, do let me see it," she said. So she was shown the egg and she began playing with the coach, wheeling it up and down along the desk.

"Oh no, no, please don't do that, it's *far* too valuable," one of Mr Snowman's assistants said.

"How *ridiculous*," Aunt Titti replied, "I used to play with this in the nursery!"

Indeed, I remember how I used to play with a Fabergé pig in the nursery bathroom. It had ruby eyes and was rather beautiful – it used to be an ashtray I think – but I used to fill it with water and have it in the bath. That was sold in the 1960s.

I also have the etching pen that Apapa used to scratch my father's name and date of birth on the window pane of the Winter Palace. It has a diamond in it that cuts through glass and a sapphire to push the diamond out to use for etching. It's not made by Fabergé but by another famous Russian jeweller.

On one of the antique panes in Pa's dressing room at Provender he etched 'Andrew' onto the glass. But I think it's no longer there. A lot of the windows had to be replaced.

Among the things I sold (and I regret that because I thought there were copies of them) were the letters between the Tsarina and Amama. They had a very close relationship when they were younger. Alexandra called herself 'Hen' and Xenia was 'Chicken'. They were just everyday letters giving news of their lives and their families.

I remember there was a solid silver pee pot with the double AA on the front and the Imperial crown, which belonged to my father. There was also the female pot, which was like a sauceboat but without the spout, which you put under your dress when needed. They were used on long journeys in the train or in the carriage.

One day when my father and his siblings were children, they were on a train with their nanny. They peed into their pots and nanny decided to empty it all out of the window. It was a hot day and everybody else had their window open, so when nanny emptied the pot out of the window, it all came back in again a few carriages down!

Anything of huge value, the icons and the few Fabergé *objets d'art,* were either hidden or in the bank but over the years they've all gone.

Father had quite a lot of Fabergé jewels and trinkets but they all had to be sold to keep the house and for everyday necessities. It was like being in Paris after the revolution all over again. There was nothing. Papa had no money at all. Mother had been keeping him for years. It wasn't a problem because she adored him, but they had to sell all his trinkets during the seventies as well as her remaining valuables. Even the personal pieces she'd inherited from McDougall and Borgström relations had to go.

She did have some fantastic things too. Papa had given her two wonderful rings. One was her beautiful sapphire and diamond engagement ring which Papa had made for her from a Fabergé brooch, and the other one was an amazing Fabergé star sapphire ring. The stone of this ring was huge; it had once been a pendant. She is wearing it on her finger in her portrait hanging in the Oak Room. Sadly both rings had to go.

There was also a picnic basket which was so heavy it took two Cossacks to carry. It was leather on the outside, wicker on the inside – it had full sized plates and silver and crystal decanters. It was sold at Sotheby's in London in 1975. I can't remember how much it went for, but within a week it was on sale in New York for three times the amount! I have a photo of Alexander III and Dagmar in a carriage with this basket, which was used for picnic lunches for the family.

When my half-sister Mysh died in France she left her Romanov pieces to my two half brothers because she was really ill latterly. I hadn't seen her for some time, but we used to see each other quite a lot. She died in October 2000, six months after Mother. There was a bad relationship between step-mother and step-children; Mother had been a step-child too.

So most of Mysh's Romanov jewellery and objets d'art went to Andrew, including the Fabergé bracelet which had been made for Amama when she'd had her first son, my father. The date of January 25th 1897 was set in rubies and diamonds all the way round. Mysh had told me that she would give to it me, or give it to my daughter, before she died. But because she was so ill she was unable to do so.

The bracelet was sold. Sadly, it went for very little – I think it was $16,000. Afterwards I was told: "Oh, the buyer will keep it for you until you can afford to buy it". $16,000 then was about £9,000 so it was too much for me. Still, it wasn't that much for such a well documented Fabergé bracelet.

In the 1950s a man called Herbert Galloway Stewart wrote to me. He had been tutor to Pa and his brothers from 1908 until the revolution. I wasn't given his letter because I was still a child but it was enclosed in one of two decorative boxes that the Tsar's daughters had made in captivity. I wasn't given either of them until I was about twelve or thirteen, by which time Herbert Stewart was dead. They were always kept in a cupboard so they couldn't get damaged and I couldn't play with them.

I still have the letter that Xenia wrote to Queen Victoria in 1894, thanking her for the wedding present. "Your Majesty… I hope you will not mind me writing these few lines of grateful thanks for the lovely present you so kindly sent to me for my wedding. It touched me deeply. We are so happy to have *Dearest* Aunt Alix [the later Queen Alexandra] and the cousins here…"

I also have some interesting correspondence between my great-grandmother Dagmar and her nephew Grand Duke Kyrill, eldest son of Alexander III's brother Grand Duke Vladimir who had died in 1909.

Pa said that there was an unwritten agreement by which no member of the Imperial family would claim the throne while the Dowager Empress was alive. Therefore, as the senior survivor of the Romanov family, my great-grandmother was outraged when in 1924, as soon as her sons Tsar Nicholas and Grand Duke Michael were declared legally dead, Kyrill issued a manifesto declaring that from 31 August 1924 he had assumed the title of Emperor.

Dagmar had never forgiven him for marching to the Duma (the Russian parliament) with his regiment in 1917. She didn't believe her sons were dead and she condemned his assumption of the 'throne' as premature. She was even more annoyed at not hearing the news in advance from Kyrill, but learning about it from the newspapers. She immediately sent a telegram to Grand Duke Nicholas Nicolaievich, cousin of the Tsar and former Commander-in-Chief of the Russian Army. The telegram exists in a draft version in French:

TELEGRAM.

DEN DANSKE STATSTELEGRAF

Grand Duc Kyrill Cobourg
I deplore that yr letter
arrived same day as I read
your declaration in papers.
My only answer is that as I
am convinced that my two
beloved sons are alive I consider
yr act premature as unfair
accompli.
Aunt Minny

Telegram from the Dowager Empress ('Aunt Minny') to Kyrill, 1924.

TELEGRAM.

DEN DANSKE STATSTELEGRAF

Sautenay

Grand Duc Nicolas. Choigny (France)
Viens d'apprendre avec étonnement
action de K.W. Déplore nouveau
grand trouble que cela mettra
parmi tous les émigrés. Que
comptes tu faire?

Telegram from the Dowager Empress to Grand Duke Nicholas, 1924.

To Grand Duke Nikolai, Choigny.

Have just learned with astonishment of K.V.'s action. Deplore great new trouble that this will cause among all the emigrants. What do you think should be done? Marie.

She then sent a telegram to Kyrill, the draft of which has also been preserved. The last sentence originally said, 'I consider your act as premature.

To Grand Duke Kyrill, Coburg.

I deplore your letter arrived same day as I read your declaration in papers. My only answer is that as I am convinced that my two beloved sons are alive I can't look upon your action as un fait accompli. Aunt Minny [the Empress's family name].

After his proclamation Kyrill wrote to my great-grandmother asking for her blessing. On 4 October she replied from Hvidøre:

Dear Kyrill
I am sending you my answer to your letter. In asking me for my blessing, you evidently didn't need, nor expect it as you never waited. You can see by my enclosed telegram, that you even gave me no time to answer.
    You can imagine my feelings when I read the whole thing in the papers.
    Think of the false position you have put yourself in & all the others & the disquiet you have sown in so many minds and hearts.
    God bless us!
    Your affectionate & sorrowful Aunt Minny.

The following week she received a long letter from Kyrill in which he tried to explain his actions.

Villa Edinburgh, Coburg. 11 October 1924.

Dear Aunt Minny
Your letter of 4th has only reached me today. I am very sorry to have upset you so much. Indeed I did hope for & expect your blessing. It was by some unpardonable indiscretion, by no means coming from me, that the news appeared in the foreign papers without giving your answer time to reach me. Since four years I have had but one wish to see & consult with you, but have always received the answer that you wished to see none of us & that you

Hvidøre. Sept. 21 / Oct 4 24.

Dear Kyrill

I am sending you my answer to yr letter: [...]

Letter from the Dowager Empress ('Aunt Minny') to Kyrill, 1924.

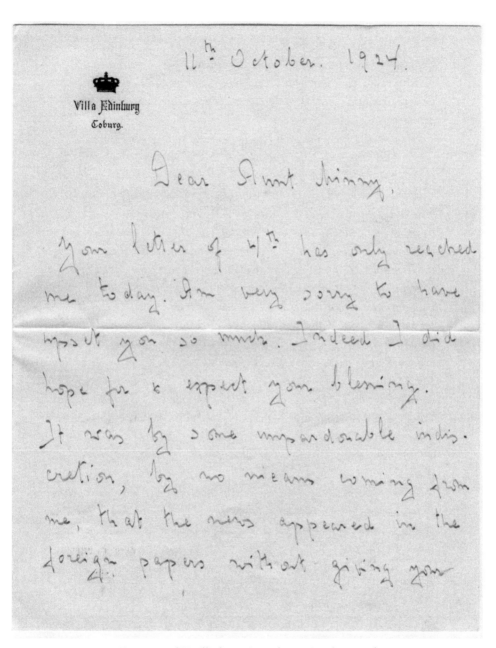

11th October. 1924.

Villa Edinburg
Coburg.

Dear Aunt Minny,

Your letter of 4th has only reached
me today. Am very sorry to have
upset you so much. Indeed I did
hope for & expect your blessing.
It was by some unpardonable indiscretion, by no means coming from
me, that the news appeared in the
foreign papers without giving you

First page of Kyrill's letter in reply, 11 October 1924.

desired to be left out of all political discussions. Now that I have been obliged, as you know, with a heavy heart to take this great step, you announce that you believe your sons are still living. Is it possible that with such a hope in your heart you have during all these years taken no measures to liberate them from their possible hiding place nor to communicate to me your reasons for not doing so.

Now that I have declared myself Emperor you by Nicholasha's advice consider my step 'premature' saying that it will be time enough to settle all this in Russia! Thereby trying to oppose any active work for the liberation of Russia. I can only repeat that I consider it my sacred duty to stand at the head of a united movement to save our Country. I swear to you that I will do all in my power to find your sons for you, if they're still alive, but till then I must act as if they were no more existing & will hoist, with full right the Emperor's Standard & bear the title until I can lay it at their feet. In no other way can we unite all our true thinking people in & outside Russia. I cannot believe that rather than see another man, myself in this instance, take up your sons' duties, you side with Nicholasha who proved himself in the past a traitor through & through to Nicky & who continues his destructive work up to the present moment. From so many talks with you & Xenia I know how entirely you shared this point of view. You knew that Nicholasha was in the hands of the 'black women' (as you used to call them), [Grand Duchesses Anastasia and Miltiza Nicolaievna, wives respectively of Grand Dukes Nicholas and Peter Nicolaievich] *used as the instrument of secret forces & societies aiming at the downfall of all empires & Christianity itself. You have seen them at work slowly & surely destroying Nicky, Alix & the Church, introducing Philippes & Rasputins to undermine their prestige. In former days you yourself have fought them day & night. In the end Nicky was fully aware of this himself, as you know, when he removed him from the supreme command. The very popularity that Nicholasha is still supposed to possess is trumpeted abroad by those very same destructive agents who wish to discredit any 'monarchique' movement.*

Therefore I will never admit a movement headed by liars. Having fully explained all this to you I once more ask you for your blessing as my designs are absolutely pure & my loyalty to the remembrance of yours Sons & Grandson remains inébranlable [steadfast].

I will await your answer and remain always
your deeply & truly devoted Kyrill.

152

Kyrill never received the Dowager Empress's blessing and his action split the monarchist movement. She denounced him publicly in a letter to Grand Duke Nicholas Nicolaievich published at her request in the *New York Times*. There were other Romanov letters and documents at Provender, but I've had to sell them in order to restore the house and pay my bills.

12

REFLECTIONS

THE FIRST TIME I went to Russia was in July 1998 for the burial of the Tsar and his family. I went with my son Fran, who had just come back from South Africa a few months before. He had hair below his shoulders and looked more like my 'minder' than my son – which was quite useful of course!

It was an incredible experience. Although my father never really talked about Moscow he had spoken a lot about St Petersburg, which he adored. He particularly loved Gatchina, which is a huge palace about 30 miles outside St Petersburg. It was his favourite palace because they stayed there with Dagmar and it was large enough to accommodate all the family comfortably.

As we came into the city on the luxury coaches that had been organised, it felt like home. It was an amazing feeling to look around and see this place that he had told me so much about, a strange feeling. I just *love* Petersburg, there's something so magical about it. But I didn't find it upsetting being there because I wasn't around when all the tragedies happened.

To meet members of the family I hadn't seen since I was a child, or had never met at all, was also wonderful. We all met at the Astoria Hotel. Fran and I couldn't get into the Astoria as they were already booked up, so we stayed on a ship along the river called the Peterhof Ship. We had to go to the hotel every morning, because all the coaches left from the Astoria.

My cousin Dmitri, whose funeral I've just been to in Denmark, had been in Ekaterinburg, and he'd supervised the loading of the coffins of the Tsar and his family onto the massive transport plane. When they arrived at Pulkova Airport in St Petersburg we were all standing on the

154

red carpet with the band. The Queen had sent four officers and a piper from the Royal Scots Dragoon Guards, formerly the Royal Scots Greys, because Nicholas II had been Colonel in Chief of the Scots Greys.

The huge plane arrived next to us, so close and so well piloted, and they took the coffins off one by one, in reverse order of priority. First came the cook, then the maid, followed by the valet and the doctor, then the children in order of age and then finally the Tsarina. Up until then Russian troops had been carrying the coffins with senior officers being the pall bearers of the Tsarina's coffin. Finally the Scots Greys brought out Tsar Nicholas.

They were very small coffins, almost child sized. They were all put into identical green transit vans which had been made into hearses. I think they had the crest on the side; there was something distinctive about them.

We followed them all the way into St Petersburg and it was interesting to see the reaction of the crowds which were *huge*. People were all making the sign of the cross as the coffins moved past. We were all quite surprised.

When we arrived at the SS Peter & Paul Fortress they had to unload the coffins to walk over the bridge, and the piper from the Scots Greys piped them in all the way to the cathedral. It was all very moving. Then they lay in state and a long service followed.

No one seemed to know whether President Yeltsin was going to turn up for the actual funeral the next day. It was only that night that he told my cousin Nicholas, the head of the Romanoff family, that he *would* be coming.

The next day President Yeltsin and his entourage appeared in the cathedral. I'd popped into the Ladies just before the service started and only got back into place about thirty seconds before the door was shut. Otherwise I'd probably have missed it all. My God, that service was long! I didn't understand a word either, but it was very moving.

A few months ago I met the officer from the Scots Dragoon Guards who was the main pallbearer for the Tsar. I hadn't seen him since the funeral. The occasion was an intimate, private dinner for Patriarch Kyrill at the Cavalry Club. There were sixty people present and I had been invited as an 'extra' for a man whose wife couldn't come. Kyrill made a speech and the officer stood up to reply.

Later I went round the table and spoke to him. It was lovely to see him again and we had hugs and kisses all around. He said it was such an incredible event, being at the airport with the coffins of the Imperial family and then escorting the Tsar to his final resting place.

The British always manage ceremonial pomp so well, but what I had noticed about the Russian soldiers that day was that their caps were kept on with a bit of elastic under the chin. Elastic under the chin, for a man! I found that strange.

My dear cousin Rostislav, who'd had cancer but was in remission at the time, was able to attend the funeral. He kissed the floor and the coffins in the cathedral. After the funeral he went to Nantucket, Massachusetts to see his mother, and was taken ill. He'd had a cold when he was in St Petersburg but it became worse after he arrived in America.

At first they thought it *was* just a cold. But it seems that at some point between the time he was in the cathedral in St Petersburg and when he got to Nantucket, he had ingested something that mimicked the symptoms of his cancer. He spent quite a while in hospital in one of the big towns near there, possibly Boston, and then he was flown back to the Royal Marsden Hospital in London. The cancer killed him the following year. That was very sad, and awful for his children.

My daughter Poggy and I had a couple of days to explore St Petersburg while the rest of the family went on a cruise to a holy island, so we decided to visit the Yusupov Palace by the Moika Canal. It had been the Yusupovs' main St Petersburg home and was one of the places Felix returned to just after the revolution to hide the family treasures, including many of Aunt Titti's jewels. Unfortunately, his hiding places were later discovered by the Bolsheviks.

The entrance to the palace was very dark and as we walked in it didn't have a very good feeling. Perhaps it was the dark stained wood on the staircase combined with the lack of light. The staff spoke practically no English, so we each rented an audio cassette guide with headphones.

As we toured the palace, Poggy turned to me and said that she didn't like the place at all. We were walking down a long corridor and she had got ahead of her cassette because she wanted to get out as quickly as possible. But we had to follow the arrows indicating the route of the tour.

When we entered the theatre, we were stunned by the opulence of the room. It was truly magnificent. But as we walked towards the stage, we both began to feel very sick. We turned back and decided to visit the loo, which was in the basement. By now the cassette was still covering the first room, whereas we had covered the majority of the rooms which were open. We were having a giggle about this and the fact that hardly anybody spoke English.

When we came out of the loo, we saw an arrow pointing down a narrow corridor with a closed door at the end and Poggy wanted to investigate. She was walking slightly ahead of me, and as she got closer to the door she began to look very green. She stopped and waited for me.

By the time I caught up with her I too felt physically sick. Neither of us could take a step forward. We turned back and decided to find someone who spoke English. When we got back to the entrance Poggy asked what had happened in the basement. We were told that this is where Felix had tried to poison Rasputin with cakes and wine before shooting him. Until our visit, Poggy had no idea that this was the palace where Rasputin was murdered.

In fact we now know that Rasputin crawled up a small back stairway from the basement and through a side door to a courtyard at the front, where he was finally murdered. But Poggy and I certainly had an unpleasant experience and felt a spirit there.

Of course I visited the Hermitage Museum, which used to be the Tsar's Winter Palace. Pa said there was a garden on the Winter Palace roof. It was quite a decent sized one too.

I was naturally very anxious to see the room in Nicholas II's private apartments where Pa was born. The guides had no idea that my father was born there and didn't seem to be aware that Apapa had etched the details on the window pane. When I walked to the window, I burst into tears. There, etched into the glass, was Apapa's signature with my father's name and the date of his birth just like I had been told. It had miraculously survived the revolution and the Second World War! *That* made me cry, and I remember Fran, who was nineteen at the time, saying, "Get a *grip*, Mum!"

The signature is on the inside. The windows have an early type of double-glazing, with an outer window pane and, on the inside, there are shutters, but they're made of glass. The family used that etching pen to scratch on window panes all over Russia in every palace.

The second time I visited the room, the inside glass door of the window had been swapped for one on which the Tsarina had written: '1902. Alicky looking at the Hussars.' So nowadays there's the pane my grandfather wrote on and another on which the Tsarina had written. It's Alexandra's one that tourists are usually shown. It's re-writing history in a way, but I suppose Papa isn't well-known enough today for visitors to understand the significance of that pane and the history of the room. Luckily, I've seen Apapa's window pane twice.

In 2006 the remains of my great-grandmother Dagmar were taken from Denmark and reburied in Russia, according to her last wishes. We went to see her remains leave Denmark, staying at the Admiral Hotel in Copenhagen with many other members of the family.

The evening before the big memorial service we were all supposed to go to Roskilde Cathedral for the removal of her body from the crypt to the nave. I was given a lift by Anna von Lowzow, who drove me there very quickly to Roskilde.

And thank God for Anna! I was virtually the only one to turn up at Roskilde. Our crowd were all drinking and rolling around at the hotel and they didn't think it was important. Only Dmitri, his wife Dorrit and Paul Kulikovsky and his wife were there. We were all *meant* to be there but, Dmitri hadn't made this clear – he had just presumed everybody else would realize they should be present. "Thank Goodness you came," he said.

The service was very moving. There was something almost surreal about bringing up the Empress's body from the crypt and seeing the yellow flag on the coffin. Her body was taken up to the nave and the next day there was a big memorial service, attended by Queen Margarethe and other members of the Danish royal family. Then they put the coffin onto a horse-drawn hearse, which was taken through the streets of Copenhagen to the quay where a new gunboat was waiting. Dmitri, Dorrit and Paul Kulikovsky went on board.

The coffin was lead lined and it had a marble slab underneath so it weighed a ton. They were trying to put it into the gunboat but it wouldn't quite fit, so suddenly a naval or army officer, a very good looking Dane, gave it an extra push with his boot! My God, those Danish officers were so good looking! All the young girls, even the old girls, were just drooling over them in Russia.

Before I left Denmark, I unveiled the plaque for a new square in Copenhagen, called Kejserinde Dagmars Plads in honour of my great-grandmother. Then we flew to St Petersburg.

Meanwhile Dagmar went on the gunboat to Kronstadt naval base near St Petersburg where the coffin was transferred to a Russian ship. Then they continued to Peterhof, where she lay in state in a little chapel in the park. I remember going to kiss the coffin. The queues went way back, it was incredible how many people wanted to pay their respects to her.

The funeral service was held in St Isaacs Cathedral. I'd never been there before. It was stunning, with all the candles, the pillars, the malachite and the lapis lazuli – it was just breathtaking. It's reverted to being a museum now and I've been back a couple of times but it didn't have the same atmosphere – it's much darker now. On the day of the funeral it was so light and bright. There must have been over fifty priests there. My daughter, who thought priests should maintain a certain decorum, was horrified when some of them took out cameras and started photographing the coffin.

After the service coaches took us from St Isaacs to the SS Peter & Paul Fortress, where we had to walk across the bridge.

When we were standing in the SS Peter & Paul Cathedral for the final burial service, the Romanov group stood in one section of the cathedral, while the King of Greece, Prince Michael of Kent and various other people were placed in another section. Dmitri and Nicholas kept prodding me in the back to keep me at the front, saying, "You're the nearest relative."

With so many dignitaries attending, there was some concern about the possibility of bombs and attacks. One of the Danish entourage was star gazing and he was so busy looking up at the ceiling that he didn't see the grave – and he fell into it with a bang! The noise was so loud that it startled everybody, and I saw a lot of people ducking. He was quickly pulled out but apparently left his mobile phone down there. It could be heard ringing after the grave was filled in. Luckily, he was fine although as the grave was stone it must have hurt him a bit.

I heard later that when they went to dig Dagmar's grave to place her next to her husband they found it had already been dug. It had obviously been prepared before the revolution when Alexander III was buried, so that she could eventually be laid beside him.

After the reburial we had a huge wake in the Ethnographic Museum but it was cut short because Mary of Denmark was in the early stages of pregnancy, although this wasn't common knowledge yet, and she became sick. (She'd already left St Isaacs for a brief period because she felt unwell.) Once Mary and Frederik left *we* all had to leave, as protocol demanded. So we only had the first course. Shortly afterwards came the *official* news that Mary was expecting another baby.

Whenever I've been to St Petersburg or to Moscow, it's been in a huge group and for a purpose – a funeral, a reburial or something – so I hadn't wandered off piste at all. But about six years ago I went to Ekaterinburg with my daughter. It was early December, the temperature was minus thirty-one, our nasal hairs froze and we had scarves across our faces every time we went out.

We walked from the hotel to the Church of Blood in Honour of All Saints Resplendent in the Russian Land, which stands on the site of the Ipatiev House. It was probably less than a quarter of a mile away but it seemed much further. The snow had been piled up on the pavements about eight foot high on both sides, there was blue sky and sunshine but it was bitterly cold.

We got to the church and looked around on the ground level, then went down into the crypt, which is the basement where the Tsar and his family were murdered. It was very moving and particularly interesting to my daughter and I, who can feel and sometimes see the supernatural.

There was no-one there who spoke English but eventually they managed to understand who I was and they got frightfully excited. They said "please come back tomorrow, because we want to do a video and we'll have somebody to interpret."

So we came back at eleven o'clock the next morning. They took us to the priest's house, where they gave us tea with jam in, which we thought rather strange, and lots of cakes and delicacies to eat. I didn't feel well, so I didn't go to the place where the Tsar's bones were found and where they've now built the wooden churches, one for each of them. My daughter went, but there's only one road in and out and the amount of traffic was amazing. Although it's not far, it took her four hours to get back by taxi!

I've been to Moscow three or four times. I loved the Kremlin, the churches are wonderful, especially the Assumption Cathedral where for over three hundred years the Tsars were crowned. Stepping inside the Kremlin's walls felt as if I was transported back to the days of Imperial Russia.

I don't like the feel of Moscow though. It doesn't have the same feel good factor as St Petersburg. I find it too commercial and it appears to be oozing with flashy people. I've been there in winter with my daughter, and we've also been to St Petersburg in winter, all on the same trip. Otherwise, I don't go unless I'm invited. Everybody is very nice to us.

There are still the remains of Alexei and Maria to bury. I think it might take place in 2018 or the year after. Or maybe never. The Patriarch is one of the people holding it up. It was cancelled three times in 2016, which was unfortunate.

We had been warned by the Russian Embassy not to get our tickets in advance but to wait for the go-ahead. However, because there were good deals on British Airways and at the Astoria, we all booked our tickets, including my son Nick and his wife Jude. He'd never been to Russia. He was in the RAF at the time of the other burials and his job was sensitive, so he wasn't allowed to go. We all bought our tickets and then the burial was cancelled, so we all lost out.

Then there were rumours that it was going to go ahead on another date, but it too was cancelled.

The Patriarch and President Putin gave orders to dig up virtually all the crypt of Nicholas and his family to take DNA samples to prove they are the genuine remains. They then did the same for Dagmar and then Alexander III. The Communists had let my great-grandfather rest in peace. It's a shame he wasn't shown the same respect by others.

People have gone berserk over the authenticity of these remains, but we are convinced they *are* who the experts said they were. It's now become a political nonsense. I suspect that the burial of Alexei and Maria might be planned for 2018 to correspond with the centenary of their murders.

It now appears that they've also found the body of Tsar Nicholas's brother Michael who was shot by the Bolsheviks in the woods outside Perm, but for a long time nobody knew where. Then about five years ago Michael's body was found down a mine, along with that of his secretary Johnson, who was in fact more of a friend than a secretary.

I only heard about this discovery because a Russian man, I think he was a historian, came to Provender on one of the tours. Then somebody else also told me, I think it was someone from the Russian Embassy. The Russians were not expecting to find the bodies and there was no provision to rebury them anywhere, so they didn't know what to do with them. The discovery has been kept very quiet because the whole thing was quite accidental. DNA tests have established the identity of the bodies, but I don't know what happened to them after that.

I'm involved in The Romanoff Family Association, being the junior member of the senior generation. All my first cousins are dead now except Marina. There were lots of them and they were all roughly the same age, so they became a little group. They formed the Family Association in Paris in the seventies, I believe, with some members of the second generation part of it as well.

The last meeting we had was held in the Cottage at Peterhof, which was Dagmar's home on the Peterhof estate. Pa loved the Cottage. It's a charming Victorian building and there's a special room upstairs which my father used to absolutely wax lyrical about. It's a lovely room and in summer the walls concertina back to let the sun in. My father told me so much about it that when we had the Family Association meeting there, the first one I'd been to, I was really fascinated. My son Fran meanwhile was downstairs. He got under the rope and sat in his great-grandfather's chair. He was soon ousted!

Nobody knows who is going to be head of the Romanoff Family Association now. My cousin Nicholas died in 2014 and his brother Dmitri died in early 2017. My half-brother Andrew is 95. He has three sons but they're very Americanised. The oldest one, Alexei, who is three years younger than me, speaks fluent Russian because his mother was Russian but neither he nor his half-brother Peter has any heirs. Only the youngest boy, the baby Andrew, has a daughter who is in her twenties now. When I said to them, "You know there's still time to breed a son," they replied, "Oh no, we got so teased at school about being princes I wouldn't want to wish that on another boy."

There was never any involvement in events; the Association was just for fun, to keep tabs on who was doing what amongst the family, but it has no great significance. However the Romanov Fund for Russia, which Dmitri ran, is altogether different and he did a lot of good work for it. President Putin gave him an honour last year; he received a medal and other recognitions for his services.

My young cousin Misha has taken it over now and his brother Nikita and sister Alexandra are also involved. They are my cousin Rostislav's children and Misha was one of the pallbearers at Dmitri's funeral in January 2017. The three of them are quite capable of organising the Fund, so all should run smoothly.

I'm also patron of various balls, so I'm offered free accommodation and complimentary tickets. Four of them are associated with Russia. They can be great fun but it does rather depend on who's there and who you're sitting next to. But it's really about meet and greet, smile sweetly and be polite.

It can be quite amusing when at least one of my children comes with me, because there's always one of these "*Mum!* You can't say that!" moments. They're less embarrassed about me now though. But I *can* embarrass them enormously.

As to the succession, I don't know. In theory, as far as blood's concerned, the next in line would be my half brother, then me and his children but it doesn't work that way. Women don't count with the

Romanovs unfortunately. We're so far down the pecking order and you can't go through the female line, so they can't inherit.

My father always said there can never be another Romanov on the throne of Russia, unless people want it, otherwise never. If anyone was put on the throne now, he'd just be a political puppet.

But Papa also said that things would eventually come right again in Russia — what goes around comes around.